HAPPY AT WORK

A Practical Guide to Overcoming Workplace Psychological Harassment

ELIZABETH CRAWFORD SPENCER
BS, MCRP, JD, PhD

HAPPY AT WORK

A PRACTICAL GUIDE TO
OVERCOMING WORKPLACE PSYCHOLOGICAL HARASSMENT

Copyright © Elizabeth Crawford Spencer

First published 2024

ISBN: 978-0-9756379-4-4

ISBN: E-Book 978-1-7635558-0-8

All rights reserved. Without limiting the rights under copyright reserved above, no part of this publication may be reproduced, stored in or introduced into a database and retrieval system or transmitted in any form or by any means (electronic, mechanical, photocopying, recording or otherwise) without the prior written permission of the owner of the copyright.

Original figures by Elizabeth Crawford Spencer

Disclaimer: The information in this book is provided for the sole purpose of commentary and is in no way intended to be used as a source of legal, accounting or any other professional advice. The providers of this information assume no responsibility or liability whatsoever. The reader is responsible for obtaining their own advice and/or conducting their own research and due diligence.

Published with the assistance of Angel Key Publications
https://angelkey.com.au

Contents

Foreword vii

Preface xi

Chapter One

The path to transformation 1

Chapter Two

Do we know it when we see it? 7

    Chapter Introduction 7

    Recognising workplace psychological harassment 7

    How workplace psychological harassment happens and its impacts 13

    Chapter conclusion 24

Chapter Three

A complex constellation of relationships 29

    Chapter Introduction 29

    Who is a perpetrator 30

    What it takes to be a target 33

    The enabling silence of bystanders 37

    Chapter conclusion 40

Chapter Four

Cultures of silence at work 43

    Chapter Introduction 43

    Organisational factors that cause harassment 44

    Perverse incentives 47

    Strategies and tactics for maintaining the silence 53

    Chapter conclusion 58

Chapter Five

The secret rules 63

    Chapter Introduction. 63

    Coming to terms with where you stand and what you can expect 64

    HR/P&C accountability and motivations 70

    The suspect terrain of internal procedures. 71

    Complaints process sabotage. 74

    Navigating resolution mechanisms within complaints processes 82

    Chapter conclusion 88

Chapter Six

The legal landscape 91

    Chapter Introduction. 91

    A brief look at law and regulation around the world 91

    Law and regulation in Australia 94

    Practical tips for targets contemplating legal action 107

    Prospects for law reform 111

    Chapter conclusion 112

Chapter Seven

The target's chrysalis -victim to victor 115

    Chapter Introduction. 115

    Staying strong 116

    Maintaining perspective 121

    Intentional connection 125

    Cutting the cord. 129

    Chapter conclusion 135

Chapter Eight
Transforming workplace psychological abuse **137**
    Chapter Introduction. 137
    Recognition 138
    Response 140
    Remediation. 145
    The courage to be happy at work 147
    Chapter conclusion 154

Epilogue
The alchemy of change **157**

Foreword

Only once in my life was I ever bullied, when I was five years old. Walking a few blocks to kindergarten, a much bigger boy down the street made threatening comments and gestures. My father explained that I could avoid this by taking a different route. I was overjoyed at this clever avoidance technique.

Many people associate bullying with childhood, with young, weak, vulnerable kids at school being subject to nasty comments, humiliating demands and physical abuse. Sometimes the bullying is by an entire group. Bullying can cause lasting emotional damage.

What about adults? Surely they have mature capacities to resist the sort of harassment that occurs at schools and neighbourhoods? I started learning about adult bullying at work by talking with whistleblowers, those employees who speak out about corruption, abuse and hazards to the public. For example, an office worker alerts the boss to a discrepancy in the accounts, little knowing that it's fraud and the boss is implicated. Before long, the boss makes this poor worker's life difficult. This might be by shouting face-to-face. Or it might be criticisms at meetings in front of co-workers. Or being assigned the worst jobs, or given impossible assignments, or none at all. Sometimes it's being given the cold shoulder, not being informed of meetings and never being greeted by co-workers. The variations are great, but the common pattern is that working life becomes hell.

Whistleblowers speak out in the public interest, and it is a huge injustice that they are targeted with reprisals, including the sorts of actions that are commonly called bullying or mobbing, which is when a whole group joins in the attack. But whistleblowers are not the only targets. Anyone is potentially a victim. Sometimes it is because they are a member of an ethnic minority. Some are seen as vulnerable and hence easy targets. Some are especially competent and seen as a competitive threat. And some just happen to be in the wrong place at the wrong time: a manager is pissed off about something else and takes it out on the nearest convenient person.

Bullying is most often by someone higher in rank against a subordinate, but there are exceptions, especially with mobbing. Occasionally a group of employees will act together against a boss, for example a boss who is a woman, a member of a minority group and just someone seen as a threat to the usual order of things.

Attuned to the problem, I started reading about bullying at work. In the 1990s, this issue burst onto the scene, with books and then websites filled with stories and advice. Bullying at work has been going on for as long as people have worked together, but it took a long time before it was named and seen as a social problem.

After reading quite a few books about bullying at work, I wrote a review of them. When it came to advice about what to do, there was one depressing refrain: either put up with it or leave your job. Complaining hardly ever fixed the problem and often made it worse. Depressingly, leaving often meant co-workers would be the next victims. A boss with a pattern of harassing subordinates would pick one target, drive them out of the workplace, and then choose someone else to harass.

When it comes to bullying, things haven't changed all that much since the 1990s. In some parts of the world, bullying has been criminalised, but the obstacles facing anyone trying to use laws are enormous: financial costs are exorbitant, emotional costs are intensified, and seldom is there a positive outcome. In many workplaces, there are now policies that workers can use, but some of them are more for show than practical use.

Well, it's not all doom and gloom, because some things have changed. There is much greater awareness of the problem, and there is more written about it, and online you can find lots of information. But how can you tell what's most useful?

All I can say is that Liz Spencer's book is a worthy and useful addition to the writing on the subject. Out of the untold thousands of bullied workers, she is one of the very few to use the experience as the foundation for writing a clear-headed, informative treatment designed to help others. This is a systematic treatment by someone who knows the topic from the inside and outside. Liz has combed research for insights and presented what she's learned in clear prose, organised logically. The focus is workplaces in Australia, with wider relevance.

Several things are worthy of special mention. Liz is a lawyer, a legal academic, and she brings a lawyer's careful thinking to bear, especially in the chapter on legal responses. Secondly, Liz went through submissions to an Australian public inquiry into bullying, and intersperses quotes from submissions with her text, at appropriate places. Thirdly, she uses quotes from her personal diary in the same way. These quotes don't give details about the who and what of her experiences, but rather portray her feelings and general observations.

You can learn a lot from Liz's text about bullying. You can also learn a lot from one thing she did: keep a diary. If you're ever under threat of any kind at a workplace, or anywhere else for that matter, keep a daily record of what's happening and how you feel about it. Use Liz's diary entries as a model for how to do this. Good luck.

Emeritus Professor Brian Martin

Preface

Never doubt that a small group of thoughtful, committed people can change the world. Indeed, it is the only thing that ever has.
Margaret Mead

This book is a tool for people affected by psychological harassment at work. It shares insights about how to recognise, respond and remedy the problem, and so find ways to be happy, or at least a bit happier, at work.

Whether or not we label this a problem of epidemic proportions, the weight of research and extensive anecdotal evidence indicates the problem is extremely widespread. Precise estimates of the numbers affected vary, in part because it has not been clearly determined what we mean when we talk about psychological harassment, or its extended impacts. A certain level of certainty has been achieved regarding what is sexual harassment or physical abuse, and we no longer accept these behaviours. But the lines are anything but clear, and expectations are continually evolving around what is okay and what is not in our interactions at work. There is work to be done here.

In my own experiences of psychological harassment, I was unprepared. Too often, I was uncertain how to react when targeted, or how to help co-workers in coping with their experiences. This book brings together some of what I learned, in order to help others make sense of the perverse, protracted maelstrom that harassment can easily become. It offers supportive knowledge and guidance to targets who often feel helpless and alone. This book is also intended as a resource for bystanders and HR/P&C personnel, administrators, managers, and would-be leaders. It is for anyone who wants to better understand psychological harassment at work.

As an academic, in undertaking this project, I conducted extensive research and consultation with psychological, organisational, legal and industrial relations experts. I chose to omit the over 200 footnotes in the text, opting instead to include a list of selected references at the end of each chapter. I did this because it is my intention that the book present in a way that is as accessible as possible to a wide audience. I invite those readers who may seek further information to contact me, and to conduct your own inquiries.

The other, perhaps more important reason for omitting the extensive academic referencing is the ethnographic nature of this project as a collection of perspectives drawing upon my experiences of psychological harassment and the subsequent processes, as well as those of others as recorded in submissions to the 2012 Australian Parliamentary Inquiry into Workplace Bullying. Stories are powerful, and carry at least as much truth as other scholarly research methods. I hope readers will respect and appreciate the thoughts and feelings of others shared here, and that they will be motivated to share their own. Ideally, the full diversity of perspectives can be met with respect and open hearts.

A well-told story has its good guys and villains. But this book is not about taking sides. Human beings seek appreciation, belonging, and a sense of being valued in various ways. The discussions in these pages about perpetrators of abuse, the managers who enable them, HR/P&C's role in serving management, and bystanders who turn away are situated in the context of that shared humanity. Change takes commitment, and it requires all of us to work together. The most powerful tool discussed in this book is solidarity, and so, ultimately, this book is a call for solidarity.

Chapter One

The path to transformation

> *Coming together is a beginning. Keeping together is progress. Working together is success.*
> Henry Ford

We have learned in recent years that epidemic crises can lead to social transformation. Workplace psychological abuse infects our workplaces at great cost to individuals, organisations and society. It is one of the most serious and neglected problems in employment relations across developed economies. A Global Survey by the International Labor Organisation revealed that Australia and New Zealand have the highest reported rates of workplace violence and harassment in the world, with many respondents having suffered multiple times. The rates are higher for women, people of diverse ethnicities, faiths, physical and neurological characteristics, etc.

The quality of our working conditions matters. Over a lifetime, the average person spends over ten years at work. Most of us work to earn a living, yet for many, the 9-to-5 is much more than the 9-to-5. Work is the centre of all kinds of human interaction, for example, competition - it has long been a place of struggle and transformation - but also camaraderie, belonging, friendship, joy, and standing for what we believe in, our self-worth. For many, work is deeply connected to who we are.

Work integrates our sensibilities around social and environmental issues and our overall identity and lifestyle. Today, we are told, 'Bring your authentic selves to work.' But what does that mean? And are we really supposed to? The rise of social entrepreneurship and corporate social responsibility (CSR) reflects this shift toward purpose, personal fulfilment, and the opportunity to impact the world positively. In recent years, the concept of business human rights (BHR) has emerged as a new form of corporate social responsibility. It is bringing transformative change to the interface of business with human rights. In addition, the meaning of work is influenced by emerging influences such as:

- advancing technology
- the changing global economy
- the Uber economy
- intra-generational participation - sometimes four generations in a workplace simultaneously
- diversity, intersectionality, and
- a new emphasis on workplace well-being and safety.

People who find meaning and purpose in their work experience higher job satisfaction, engagement, and well-being. The modern job seeker often has the luxury of considering factors beyond salary and benefits when choosing an employer. A healthy, safe work environment attracts and retains talented employees. This means organisations prioritising mental health are more likely to enjoy greater business success, not only in relations with employees, but also with shareholders, customers, suppliers, and other stakeholders. Relational capital across-the-board is the beneficiary of happier workplaces.

COVID and the working from home phenomenon have reinforced the importance of ensuring that the work environment is safe and does not endanger workers' physical or psychosocial well-being. Today's workers seek employer commitment to workplaces free from psychological harassment. Mental health is a human right. Employers have a moral responsibility and a legal duty to ensure that the workplace does not threaten workers' physical or mental health. In addition to international conventions, many jurisdictions have legislation in place, as well as common law protections and social expectations.

Some workplaces model shared purpose and engagement with high levels of job satisfaction. Workers with diverse voices feel heard and respected; they are genuinely committed to values such as integrity, courage, and trust. Ideally, this will increasingly be the case in the future. Nevertheless, many employers still do not prioritise safety at work. Even while they pay lip service to values like teamwork, collaboration, openness, and transparency, it is not unusual for employers actually to incentivise and reward psychologically abusive behaviour. In many workplaces, the situation is not getting better. Often, we can't even talk about it.

Right now, workers who attend safe workplaces are the lucky ones. Despite widespread awareness of the importance of well-being, today's workplace is not always safe. Many of us still suffer demeaning and abusive treatment at work. This book is about changing that. It is about overcoming psychological harassment to transition to work environments that are safer, more productive, happier for more people.

The conversation here is not about physical violence or sexual harassment in the workplace. Those are related but distinct topics. And thankfully, sexual harassment and physical violence are now taken seriously, generally speaking. We have reached a point where, for the most part, those offences are not tolerated.

But we still let psychological harassment happen. And when we do, we deprive ourselves and each other of our right to a safe workplace. A safe shared environment in which to work is not only everyone's right, but everyone's responsibility. Solidarity of workers is a fine tradition historically. Research shows, however, that worker solidarity in recent years has declined. This decline is due to various factors, but we can turn it around. Solidarity at work is something we can embrace if we can find the courage and commitment to resist the individualistic impulse to isolate and protect ourselves, and instead make a conscious choice to support each other and to use our voices at work.

This book is not the story of any one person, but rather represents an amalgam of personal experiences and extensive research, that encompasses scholarly research as well as hundreds of accounts recorded in submissions to the 2012 Australian Parliamentary Inquiry into Workplace Bullying. Among the 319 submissions, many documented personal experiences of targets of harassment. Others were from experts in the field.

Informed by this wide range of sources, this book outlines the basics of workplace psychological harassment, offers insights and advice to manage and prevent harassment, and provides a framework for changing the conditions that allow harassment to persist and thrive, from internal processes and personal choices to broad societal transformation.

The book is organised in three parts, which represent something like a hero's journey in overcoming challenge. Taken together, it is hoped that the three parts of the book offer the reader some useful understanding, insight, and inspiration. Part One (Chapters Two and Three) introduces the phenomenon of workplace psychological harassment and the challenges it presents. This is the departure, encountering the challenge, the first ordeal in the hero's journey. Part Two (Chapters Four, Five and Six) represents the initiation. This is the second ordeal, and in this context the book describes the darkest substance, the many ways that we are tested in psychological harassment, and the obstacles in the path to overcoming its challenges. Part Three (Chapters Seven and Eight) is about ways of meeting and overcoming; this is the return, finding the courage, wisdom and strength to master ourselves in service to others.

> *Everybody can be great, because everybody can serve. You don't have to have a college degree to serve. You don't have to make your subject and your verb agree to serve....You only need a heart full of grace, a soul generated by love.*
> Martin Luther King, Jr.

Selected references

Australian House of Representatives Standing Committee on Education and Employment, Inquiry into Workplace Bullying Final Report, We Just Want It to Stop (2012) https://www.aph.gov.au/Parliamentary_Business/Committees/House_of_Representatives_Committees?url=ee/bullying/report/.

Chia, G., Lim, S. M., Sng, G. K. J., Hwang, Y. F. J., & Chia, K. S. (2019). Need for a new workplace safety and health (WSH) strategy for the fourth Industrial Revolution. *American Journal of Industrial Medicine*, *62*(4), 275-281.

Deva, S. (2021). Business and human rights: alternative approaches to transnational regulation. *Annual Review of Law and Social Science*, *17*, 139-158.

Du, S., Ma, Y., & Lee, J. Y. (2022). Workplace loneliness and the need to belong in the era of COVID-19. *Sustainability, 14*(8), 4788.

Einarsen, S. V., Hoel, H., Zapf, D., & Cooper, C. L. (Eds.). (2020). *Bullying and harassment in the workplace: Theory, research and practice*. CRC Press.

International Labor Organisation (2021) Global Survey. Lloyd's Register Foundation World Risk Poll.

Liu, C. (2021). *Virtue hoarders: The case against the professional managerial class*. University of Minnesota Press.

Potter, R. E., Dollard, M. and Tuckey, M. R. (2016) *Bullying and harassment in Australian workplaces: results from the Australian workplace barometer 2014/15*. Safe Work Australia, University of South Australia.

Pryce-Jones, J. (2011). *Happiness at work: Maximizing your psychological capital for success*. John Wiley & Sons.

Chapter Two

Do we know it when we see it?

Bullying is not just about physical violence, it's also about psychological violence – the kind of violence that leaves scars on the soul.
Julia Gillard

Chapter Introduction

Recognition of the problem is the first step to any solution. This chapter provides an overview of what workplace psychological harassment is, what it looks like, how it happens and the enormous toll it takes. It introduces the foundational concepts of harassment and the varieties of unreasonable workplace behaviours that continue to be tolerated, cultivated and rewarded. It frames workplace psychological harassment as abuse and demonstrates that it is not just the conduct of individuals, but also organisations that synergistically, exponentially compound the harm, elevating it to the level of a workplace environmental crisis.

Though individuals suffer harassment, and the harm occurs mainly at that level, it impacts everyone. The estimated cost to the economy and the psychosocial cost to individuals, families, and society is incalculable. We need greater awareness and understanding of how widespread and harmful these behaviours are and the enormous psychosocial and financial costs they exact in order to generate the necessary motivation to stop them. What is at stake is nothing less than the human right to health and personal safety.

Recognising workplace psychological harassment

While workplace violence generally is divided into physical and psychological forms of violence, the focus of this book is on workplace psychological harassment, other than sexual harassment and physical violence. Psychological harassment is the silent epidemic, estimated to be many times more prevalent than sexual harassment, but with significantly less remedial action.

In the lexicon of the modern workplace, there are many words for workplace psychological harassment. Workplace psychological abuse, psychological violence, moral harassment, bullying, mobbing – all these terms and others refer to a wide range of harmful behaviours affecting psychological well-being and performance in the workplace.

Defining the phenomenon and the need for collective agreement around it is as important as it is difficult. A US Supreme Court justice and an immortal Russian author help us connect with why psychological violence is different every time and why we need to respond as a community if we want happy workplaces.

First, Tolstoy's classic opening of *Anna Karenina*, 'Happy families are all alike; every unhappy family is unhappy in its own way', applies to working groups as much as families. We recognise this in our friendships, mentorships, and other relationships at work – we even talk of work 'husbands' and 'wives'. Like families, every workplace encounters difficult times and complex relationships. But happy, healthy organisations get through the rough patches, as do happy families. They emerge stronger and better. Unfortunately, too many organisations falter when faced with adversity, diversity, and change. There are many unhappy workplaces. And each is unhappy in its own way.

Work is ongoing to better define at a granular level the many and varied behaviours of workplace psychological abuse. They fall into several categories, including, for example, bullying, mobbing, and coercive control. The fact that there are so many overlapping and unclear categories of psychological violence makes it difficult to begin to address them effectively. How we describe, define, and collectively understand harassment is crucial. Until we are clear about what we are talking about, we can never adequately address the problem.

Bullying is the repeated and persistent aggressive behaviour that may be verbal, psychological, or physical in nature, directed towards an individual or a group. Bullying in the workplace has been described as an act of domination through an abuse of power, a psychosocial aggression in which the perpetrator plans and implements a destabilisation of the position of another. The features of bullying as a distinct phenomenon include repetition, duration, escalation, harm, attributed intent, hostile work environment, power disparity, communication patterning and distorted communication networks.

Bullying can be abusive or offensive language, insults, ridicule, sarcasm or intimidating remarks, or it may take the form of spreading derogatory innuendo or rumours. It may involve teasing, pranks, threatening, abusive or offensive letters, e-mails or phone calls; inappropriate familiarity; interfering with property; repeatedly criticising or making comments intended to discredit, undermine or devalue work. Deliberately excluding someone from work-related events, social activities, or networks can be part of it, as well as deliberately withholding information or resources or supplying incorrect information. There may be inappropriate threats of dismissal, disciplinary action or demotion, unrealistic job changes, unreasonable deadlines or work assigned well below or beyond skill levels. Bullying is often controlling, with constant surveillance or over-detailed supervision and unwarranted checking of performance. Access to training and development or career opportunities can be denied without justification, aggressive behaviour, pressure to behave inappropriately, and more.

Mobbing is another commonly used term. Mobbing is the type of bullying where a group of individuals collectively harass and ostracize a target. In his seminal paper on workplace bullying, Heinz Leymann defined mobbing as 'hostile and unethical communication which is directed systematically by one or several persons mainly toward one individual... These actions take place often - and over a long period – and result in considerable psychosomatic and social misery'. Mobbing may include verbal abuse, spreading rumours, social isolation, undermining work performance, sabotaging projects, repeated criticism, humiliation, and exclusion. The persistent, deliberate, and repeated mistreatment of both bullying and mobbing typically creates a hostile and stressful environment for the target, often resulting in isolation and extreme stress. Consequences of mobbing include severe emotional distress, anxiety, depression, reduced self-esteem, and physical health problems. Leymann estimated that workplace mobbing was responsible for 15% of suicides in Sweden at that time. The overall work environment may experience increased tension, decreased productivity, and higher turnover.

A word on coercive control

Coercive control has been recognised in recent years in the domestic violence context as 'a pattern of domination that includes tactics to isolate, degrade, exploit and control a person as well as to frighten or hurt them…'. It is now an established, recognised form of domestic abuse, and is a criminal offence in the UK and Scotland. In Australia, Tasmania has criminalised some coercive controlling behaviours, with New South Wales and Queensland to follow in July 2024 and 2025 respectively. Australia also promulgates National Principles to Address Coercive Control in Family and Domestic Violence.

Abusive behaviour that involves controlling behaviours used to dominate and manipulate is common in the workplace as well. Through various tactics, such as gaslighting, isolation, threats, and intimidation, such abusive behaviour aims to instil fear, undermine self-esteem, and maintain power.

In the context of workplace psychological harassment, a manager may claim that their requirements or conditions are 'reasonable management behaviour.' Indeed, reasonable management behaviour may include setting expectations, providing constructive feedback, and guiding employees towards meeting performance standards fairly and respectfully. Reasonable management behaviour, however, should never involve tactics to manipulate, intimidate, or exert excessive control over employees' personal lives or professional decisions. It is not acceptable for anyone in a position of authority to consistently overload employees with unreasonable work, impose unrealistic deadlines, micromanage, constantly scrutinize and interfere with an employee's work, threaten, intimidate, punish or retaliate. Such behaviour is not an appropriate or ethical way to manage employees and can have severe consequences for employees' mental and emotional well-being, job satisfaction, and overall performance.

Why what we call it matters

Academic analysis has attempted to bring order to a confused subject. However, it is still a challenge to find clear and distinct definitions among the various terminologies, and definitions in the scholarly literature vary across disciplines and jurisdictions. What constitutes workplace psychological harassment depends on which term researchers use and exactly how that research defines each term.

The various forms of harassment are regarded differently depending on social and cultural context, and this adds to the difficulty in defining and managing it. Even in a given country or jurisdiction, behaving well is notoriously difficult to legislate or adjudicate. This is, however, also precisely why shared agreement on a guiding framework is so important. Because the development of an understanding of what workplace psychological abuse is (and is not) is very much about what society agrees to at any given place and time, organisational and legal rules and processes need to be structured accordingly. It is that shared understanding upon which organisational and legal rules and processes are structured and evolve.

There is still work to be done to clarify the various behaviours that will not be tolerated and how they should be dealt with. Justice Potter Stewart's famous quote, 'I know it when I see it,' underscores the challenge of a similar lack of clarity in a different context (pornography). Just as the US Supreme Court struggled with the definition of pornography in 1964, today, the lack of clarity around what is and is not workplace psychological abuse is problematic. 'I know it when I see it' may be true; nevertheless, it is a phrase that has been more criticised than lauded. Nonrational, intuitive and self-referential, it failed to provide the guiding framework society looks to courts to provide. However, Justice Stewart's famous phrase is worth noting in the psychological harassment context for two reasons.

First, it deserves credit for its courage in admitting the inadequacy of the judiciary to establish a bright line standard for subjective judgements about social norms. It is not the province of the courts to impose social standards; indeed, it is dangerous for them to do so. As legal scholar James A. Henderson, Jr. wrote (this time in the context of negligence), 'We are rapidly approaching the day when liability will be determined routinely on a case by case, 'under all the circumstances' basis, with decision-makers… guided only by the broadest of general principles. When that day arrives, the retreat from the rule of law will be complete, the principled decision will have been replaced with the decision by whim, and the common law will have degenerated into an unjustifiably inefficient, thinly disguised lottery' and exposing courts to 'unadjudicated problems of social planning'.

The second related point is that 'I know it when I see it' is not the abdication it may seem, but rather implies a recognition of the importance of subjective and non-rational elements in policy and decision-making around behavioural norms, including civility in the workplace. 'I know it when I see it' does not invoke a captain's call. Instead, the guiding framework to prevent and stop harassment requires a shared understanding of what we seek to curtail.

There are many other reasons why the law and legal recourse do not present a very satisfying path in addressing bullying in the workplace, and these reasons will be more fully discussed in the section on legal recourse. The main point here is that workplace bullying is a social issue that is best understood and dealt with as a social problem rather than through legal channels.

The question remains - how are we to arrive at a collective conscience that we can live with through processes for formulating and acculturating collective community standards that do not drift toward the tyrannical? We can and must credit the lived experience and beliefs of others, acknowledging also that all human truths are partial. This is an increasingly problematic Achilles heel of a highly individualistic cultural ethos. A guiding framework for freedom to express our opinions in the workplace can be derived from principles found in the law, both public and private. However, those principles must still be informed by agreement about what behaviours and speech are acceptable in that context, balancing the interests of good management, transparency, collaboration, innovation, and so on.

Whatever the formula may be for a happy workplace, it is dynamic and complex and requires collective attention on an ongoing basis. Tolstoy never precisely described what he meant by a happy family. But if we could ask him today, his answer might be, 'I know it when I see it.'

How workplace psychological harassment happens and its impacts

'Workplace bullying is a pandemic ... characterised by misuse and abuse of power, lack of cultural leadership and awareness from the top of institutions and organisations, reflected in huge economic, social and personal loss ….'

Submission 35

Because harassment can take many forms, there is no one identifiable pattern and no formula for decisively determining what is going on. It can be difficult to know for sure who is doing it, when it's happening, and why. Because each unhappy workplace is unhappy in its own way, there are countless stories and entire books, blogs and podcast series devoted to these stories.

It can be subtle or patently obvious, but harassment is always a persistent pattern that undermines the target's sense of competence and self-worth. It exerts power and control through tactics designed to manipulate thoughts, beliefs and perceptions. Verbal or non-verbal, it can include gaslighting, undermining, sabotaging, gossiping, isolating, denigrating and/or defaming, to name a few. Whatever forms it may take, harassment creates a psychological work environment akin to being under siege.

Because there is not one clear definition or classification of precisely what workplace psychological harassment is and isn't, when and where it happens, and how, the classifications of the various behaviours can be almost endless. Whether behaviour is or is not harassment depends on the situation, but a common theme is that the impacts of harassment register intensely and deeply with targets and their networks, who pay a high price personally and professionally. The psychosocial ramifications can be devastating, affecting not only the individual but family and friends and relationships in all aspects of life.

Research shows that harassment is typically an escalating process. Glasl's model of conflict escalation differentiates among three phases and nine stages. The first phase is 'rationality and control,' the second 'severing the relationship,' and the third 'aggression and destruction.' Zapf and Gross found five different patterns of bullying; most participants reported that bullying escalated over time.

Thus, 'I know it when I see it' doesn't happen immediately. It may take some time for the target to realise that what is going on is more than just mismanagement, ineptitude or the clumsy recklessness of a new, untrained, stressed or grumpy manager. 'A malignant cancer... [that] creeps up on you long before you – or anyone else - can appreciate what it is...', it progresses 'from subtle low-level aggression to bullying to stigmatisation and finally to traumatisation – diminishment or destruction.' Neither linear nor predictable, the pattern may include sabotaging, stonewalling, denigration, taking credit for the work of others, undermining, gossiping, incivility and tactics to silence staff over time.

As harassment unfolds in steps or stages, the boundaries of the stages overlap, spiral and fold in on themselves, creating an uneven chronology of experience that can often feel manic. The early stage is, in some ways, the most damaging time in the harassment process, when the target is still trusting and so most vulnerable. The perpetrator has the element of surprise; can plan, create alliances, and undermine more easily at this point, rather than later when the target is alert to the behaviours and may be keeping records and trying to garner support.

> *I was told that with my manager, 'you're either in the locker room or you're out'. No middle ground. He used sporting metaphors a lot and patted the guys on the back and it was all good fun. But not with me. I felt covert sexual aggression. It wasn't just interfering with my personal things, such as toying with my glasses case in a meeting, or taking a sip from my coffee. It was the way he said my name, a coy way of pretending a familiarity that didn't exist. But no one else seemed to notice, and what could I prove?*
>
> Personal diary

The target begins to question everything, most especially and damagingly themselves. Confidence erodes. Even when the target knows what's happening, they usually have little or no experience defending against such attacks. While they are told there is support, in practice, they will discover that there may be some counselling, but for the most part, the workplace closes ranks against them. They feel they have nowhere to turn.

While targets are often 'bullied down' by someone higher up in the organisation, there is also a very real likelihood of being 'bullied up' when others become aware that targets are vulnerable, out of favour, isolated and destabilised. For various reasons, colleagues can be led to engage in unethical behaviour, particularly in stressed and uncertain organisations, where factionalism is already rife. The target will likely become distressed at this stage as they comprehend how their reputation, livelihood and relationships have all been damaged, perhaps irreparably.

In the later stages of the harassment process, something happens that makes it clear that the target can no longer ignore, stay under the radar and/or 'ride it out'. They are pushed into a corner and feel forced to act. By this time, the target may have begun to detect a strategy researchers call DARVO (Deny, Attack, and Reverse Victim and Offender). The perpetrator uses DARVO tactics to debilitate the target further. If the target speaks up, the perpetrator accuses the target of making false accusations and attacks the target's character and credibility.

Potentially most distressing for targets is that the employer not only fails to provide support but actually sides with the perpetrator, engaging in a form of institutional DARVO and tactics of outrage management. The unhealthy behaviours that the target has summoned the courage to identify are ignored, minimised and/or denied. We will examine how and why this happens in Chapter Four, but first, as part of recognising the phenomenon of harassment, it is important to appreciate its impacts.

How harassment impacts the target

Intent does not play a big role in defining harassment, *but impact does*. While the significance of intent in psychological harassment has some fascinating implications, they are beyond this volume's scope. The focus here is on what researchers in psychology say matters most - the effect. Harassment damages the target's emotional state, self-esteem, confidence, and sense of self-worth.

No matter how harassment plays out over time, at each stage, the onus of identifying and calling out the behaviour is on the target, and the compounding pressure puts increasing strain on their mental health, as well as that of their family and friends, bystanders and the workplace. Once a target recognises harassment for what it is, they may go through stages of grief - denial, anger, bargaining, depression, and acceptance.

There was a lot of pressure. I had finally understood I was under attack. I told my manager I needed support. People I was supposed to be managing sensed 'blood in the water'. He said he didn't like that phrase. Neither did I.

Personal diary

The Leymann Inventory of Psychological Terror (LIPT) provides a typography of effects. Perpetrators become adept at tailoring psychological harassment to achieve maximum impact in the particular circumstances for that particular target. These include effects on self-expression and communication, social contacts, personal reputation, occupational situation, and quality of life, as well as physical person, property, and/or health.

Psychological harassment is a significant predictor for subsequent mental health problems. Causing even a few of the effects on Leymann's list may be enough to lead to depressive anxiety, post-traumatic stress disorder (PTSD) and other stress-related psychological complaints. Targets feel excluded, singled out and otherwise disadvantaged. Their credibility is questioned; they are the subject of inappropriate comments; are made to feel unwelcome, not part of the team; are subjected to unequal conditions and requirements; are found to have faults more often than others; given unequal censure; and are more highly scrutinised.

For many, the workplace is a social environment central to the quality of everyday life in which identity, social interaction, and basic human needs are intertwined. Because it inhibits the ability of individuals to meet basic human needs, psychological harassment leads directly to adverse consequences for targets; it is linked to a host of physical, psychological, organisational, and social costs. Targets experience isolation and shame, may lose their employment or have their employability negatively impacted and experience mental health and/or physical crises.

If they respond, targets are susceptible to more criticism. They are labelled as aggressive, lacking executive presence, not fitting the culture, etc. This can be the start of mobbing, DARVO, bystander betrayal and institutional betrayal – with the added stress these may bring.

Whether or not advisable, it is not uncommon to have close personal and even intimate relationships connected with work. And it can be doubly devastating when psychological harassment destroys, not only one's working life and professional standing, but also these significant personal relationships.

Stress

The predominant health effect associated with harassment at work is stress. The negative effects of stress correlate with poor mental and physical health. Many targets experience depression, anxiety and stress-related illnesses. One study found that up to 77% of targets experience PTSD, and another found the effects similar to those caused by child abuse. The effects are cumulative; throughout the harassment process, conflict residues map onto the accumulative model of stress.

> *I have suffered bad dreams, broken sleep, waking in tears and headaches since this last incident and believe that the bullying I have suffered in this office is having a detrimental effect on my health, my family and my studies.*
>
> Submission 285

The constant exposure to abusive behaviours can lead to feelings of helplessness, low self-esteem, and a diminished sense of self-worth. Targets often experience a decline in their motivation, productivity, and creativity. They may experience intrusive thoughts about the harassment or become preoccupied with the emotional impact. They may become less committed to their work and more likely to withdraw or consider leaving their job, reducing overall performance and productivity within the organisation. There is often an increase in the use of entitlements to time off from work and unpaid leave.

> *I again felt betrayed and totally alone. I was stressed and everything that was happening was starting to impact seriously on my health and family life – I was defensive all the time, did not trust anyone and felt I could not keep my emotions under control.*
>
> Submission 287

Psychological injury is physical injury, as explained by Jennifer Fraser in her book, *The Bullied Brain*. Stress-related disorders such as sleep disturbance, headaches, insomnia, high blood pressure, skin and gastrointestinal issues, musculoskeletal problems and compromised immune function are common. A recent study indicated a 59% higher risk of heart disease.

> *It is virtually impossible to remain a productive employee under these conditions. When you are the one singled out as the target, it demoralises, depresses and demotivates. Because you are isolated, it is difficult to work together with others in a productive way. It is the opposite of what we say we want in the workplace. And we turn a blind eye. In fact, we facilitate it by putting people who do these things in positions of influence over others and reinforcing that influence rather than taking them out of those positions when we discover what they are doing.*
>
> Personal diary

Isolation

> *If I want to destroy you as an individual, the best thing to do is strip you of your groups and your social identities. Take away my university, my profession, my family, my community, I am nothing.*
>
> Catherine Haslam

Targets of harassment become isolated due to intentional psychological abuse. This isolation impacts the overall work climate, impairing communication, cooperation, and teamwork. Fear of retaliation and stigma prevents targets from coming forward, from seeking help, exacerbating the damage personally, emotionally, and professionally. Additionally, targets' sense of fear, mistrust and/or lack of psychological safety increases their reluctance to seek support and collaborate with colleagues.

Suffering alone is qualitatively different and worse than suffering together. Anger, depression, and reduced self-esteem are likely to be more pronounced if the target feels they are the only person in the workplace exposed to such incivility. Isolation is a big part of why workplace psychological harassment is so painful and costly. In an era in which increasing numbers of people are living alone and/or experiencing some form of social isolation, the psychological impacts of harassment may exacerbate already existing social isolation and so result in more intense and damaging effects.

> *Unlike victims of physical work injury who get nice phone calls and 'get well' messages on a balloon, ... victims of bullying get nothing!*

> No-one contacts them, except perhaps the pay office, while their colleagues are told to keep away from them and are enabled to spread malicious rumours.... This will humiliate and devastate them further. We know that social humiliation is experienced in the same manner as a physical pain in the brain. ...It interferes with an employee's survival instinct. Thus the target is further injured.
>
> There is a growing body of research... that perception affects the injury more than the actual event. Non-violent behaviours over a period of time can be more traumatic than one physical assault. The fact is that the loss of social and professional status IS life-threatening...mean comments, social exclusion can be seen as life-threatening and have the same impact on the brain as a physical assault.
>
> Submission 58

Sabotaged belief systems

The effects are particularly profound when the target's basic belief system is a casualty of the abuse, as noted here by psychiatrist Evelyn Field:

> The reason for the severe level of permanent injury may lie in the perception and the damage to the person's belief system. The fact is that the bullying and lack of immediate validation and safety sabotages their basic, survival belief systems,... e.g. ' if they work hard, they will be respected,' 'if they ask for assistance, their employer will help', 'if they are nice, people will be nice to them,' and thus they implode, feeling helpless, powerless and lost....most targets of bullying do not believe that they deserved the bullying and are shocked when they discover what has been occurring. They are confused and then appalled when their employer, who assured them of safety and respectful conflict resolution practices, turns against them and makes everything worse, eventually forcing them out. ...I believe that once targets lose the beliefs that are core to their being, they become changed personalities. Sadly, I am unaware of any treatment that can 'put Humpty Dumpty back together again.' Most will never return to their pre-bullying personality. In addition to helping a target/victim deal with the bullying behaviours they received and/or perceived, psychological treatment also needs to help the victim cope with many different issues, including the organisational denial of bullying, retaliation by a threatened manager, betrayal and lying in court by terrified colleagues...
>
> Submission 58

Betrayal trauma

Clearly, the effects of harassment on a personal level can be devastating. For some it is a rollercoaster of terrible lows, followed by optimism that something will happen, something will change, and someone will help. But nothing changes, and no one helps.

Targets need protection in the workplace, supported with more than just, 'Here's a phone number you can call'. Just as it is wrong to leave a victim of domestic violence in a vulnerable situation, targets of harassment should be removed, or at least protected, from the source of abuse. This is especially true as targets are often cut off from any other kind of support or encouragement, victims of a hostile and unsafe work environment that the employer continues to facilitate.

More often than not, targets are left in situations where they continue to suffer abuse, even as complaints processes may be undertaken. The harassment continues and often escalates, and the betrayal of colleagues and the employer compounds it. The fact that help is not forthcoming, often the reverse, can be more painful than the harassment itself. Another aggravating phenomenon is betrayal blindness, which is the wilful refusal by others to recognise what is happening in an attempt to preserve relationships, institutions, and social systems.

> *Trust, that most essential ingredient of human relationships, becomes inaccessible; it is completely tainted and impossible to re-establish.*
>
> Personal diary

Trauma is a psychological wound, a feeling of being minimised, destabilised, and undermined, leading to the sense that a person is somehow less than who they were before, that they are not worthy. The essence of trauma is disconnection. And one blames one's self. Betrayal trauma occurs when someone who is trusted and/or who has power over a person mistreats another, for instance, when a supervisor harasses. Betrayal traumas are associated with measurable harm, both physical and mental.

> *I have been told that I have a kind of post-traumatic stress. No one is more embarrassed to use that clichéd term than me.*
>
> Submission 33

All of this often leads to career derailment and diminished professional status. Needless to say, the excerpt below was probably not written by a person who is likely anytime soon to be powering ahead in their career with clarity and confidence. Approximately 75% of targets take sick leave or extended time off work at a cost not only to the organisation, but to themselves.

> *Sitting in a cold darkened room, huddled on my sofa, cold to the bone. This is how my friend found me. Help was called for and that was the start of my journey back.*
> Submission 277

Even for those who can continue to work, it is not uncommon for harassment to lead ultimately to the target's departure from the position and the organisation and even end their career. Estimates vary, but a significant percentage of affected workers quit their jobs.

> *This experience and all that has followed has, as such, cost me life as I knew it, and changed me in every respect to my trust and relationship with employment, and a life very different and without the promise that it once held in my chosen and trained field of employment, which I personally worked very hard to achieve and was selected and trained in this position.*
> Submission 317

Wider organisational, social and economic impacts of workplace psychological harassment

The stress, isolation and destabilisation impact not only the individuals directly involved, but also bystanders, the organisation, family and community. The multiplier effect increases costs across a range of personal and social networks.

Psychosocial and financial costs of workplace psychological harassment can be far-reaching in terms of family and relationship breakdown. A destabilised target cannot interact normally and be supportive emotionally of others. Targets may lose interest in their families and even become irritable towards loved ones. Psychological harassment at work also has the potential to exacerbate or create the conditions of substance abuse and/or domestic violence at home.

Beyond the impacts on targets and their close networks, uncivil behaviour creates emotional discomfort and distress for other stakeholders, particularly bystanders. Witnessing or even being aware of harassment (or even subtle bias) can negatively affect co-workers, causing fear, stress, and emotional exhaustion, taking a toll on attitudes and decreasing cognitive and creative performance.

When harassment pervades a workplace, it is detrimental to colleagues and bystanders, impacting how teams interact and function within and outside the organisation. It creates a toxic work environment that diminishes job satisfaction and engagement and can lead to increased absenteeism and high turnover rates. The organisation's reputation may suffer, impacting its ability to attract clients, customers, and partners. The costs associated with recruiting, training, and replacing employees can also escalate.

> *Bullying in the workplace affects staff morale, motivation, engagement, (82% are disengaged at work according to a Gallop Poll of 2009) productivity, employees make mistakes, unethical behaviours and commit fraud. Bullied employees waste 10-52% of their time at work (Canada Safety Council 2000) ... half the time at work is spent 'watching your back'.*
>
> Submission 58

Harassment undermines group cohesion and performance, reducing productivity and increasing turnover. It creates a stressful environment that erodes motivation and impairs workers' ability to focus on their work. Furthermore, the stress and psychological strain can impact cognitive abilities, including decision-making and problem-solving skills. This can decrease the quality and quantity of work for the target and the entire team.

The damage caused by harassment fosters a climate of hostility and mistrust. Employees develop a sense of being undervalued, unappreciated, and demoralized. This can result in decreased effort and engagement, delays, conflicts, factionalism and impediments to achieving shared goals.

High costs also result from absenteeism and presenteeism. Most organisations would not be aware of the hidden costs associated with presenteeism and sick leave where the reason for absence is unknown. Absenteeism is the most common outcome of workplace psychological harassment. A company with 1000 employees can save an estimated $720,000 annually (at a per-employee cost of $300) by reducing its absence rate from 3% to 2%.

A range of outcomes has been identified in international research. Even using very conservative figures, each case of bullying has been estimated to cost an Australian employer around AU$17,000. One submission to the Inquiry made a rough calculation of the cost of just one aspect of workplace toxicity, triangulation, aka gossip:

> *Gossiping is a very subtle form of bullying behaviour in which people talk about (or write about) others in a manner that is negative, hurtful and belittling. Humans have a natural tendency to defend themselves and seek retribution when they feel they have been aggrieved in some way. Gossiping is taken to be an 'apparently harmless' mechanism that meets this need. However, over time this behaviour can be replaced with more overt forms of bullying. It is not difficult to imagine that every Australian worker would spend at least 10 minutes per day or approximately 1 hour per week on activities related to gossiping (face to face – such as talking and/or listening or typing/reading on social media). This means that organisations could be paying $18 billion per year for staff to spend time gossiping. Imagine if managers themselves chose not to participate in gossip and actively discouraged their team members from gossiping - instead focusing on building a constructive and open communication culture.*
>
> Submission 100

When psychological harassment occurs at higher levels of an organisation, the effects can cascade downward as 'subordinates' adopt the same behaviours and offload their aggression onto their 'subordinates'. This threatens the productivity of the entire organisation. Other miscellaneous costs to employers include unemployment insurance claims, workers' compensation, occupational stress claims, settlements or litigation, increased insurance premiums, counselling expenses, and expenses associated with professional and legal consultants.

Organisations that fail to address emotional harassment may suffer reputational damage, impacting public perception, relational capital and long-term sustainability. Working conditions characterised by low morale, poor commitment and erosion of trust will result in the most talented individuals who can easily get jobs elsewhere opting for employment with healthier and more supportive organisations. Consequently, not only the target but also bystanders leave the abusive workplace. High turnover rates mean the loss of valuable skills and knowledge, incurring costs related to recruitment, hiring, and training.

But it does not stop there. The impact of workplace psychological harassment goes beyond the organisational context and has broader consequences for society. It can result in reduced productivity, growth, and economic competitiveness. Moreover, it has implications for public health and well-being, increasing healthcare utilization and straining resources. Workplace psychological harassment erodes trust, negatively affects social cohesion, perpetuates power imbalances, and contributes to social inequality.

Precise figures are difficult to determine because of the obstacles to defining, identifying and quantifying the phenomenon and its associated effects and because harassment often goes unreported. Estimates of the total financial costs, therefore, vary widely. In 2010 the Australian Productivity Commission estimated the cost of workplace psychological harassment to be between $6 and $36 billion a year. Assuming around 10% of Australian workers are subjected to workplace violence; a 2023 study put the *minimum* annual cost to the Australian economy at approximately $30 billion.

Chapter conclusion

We cannot prevent or stop a problem unless and until we know what it is we are talking about. This chapter has described the behaviour that is harassment, as well as its effects. Until we are clear about what it is, we can never properly address the problem.

The consequences of harassment extend far beyond the immediate negative impacts suffered by individual workers, their families and social networks. Harassment impacts organisations and society more broadly by damaging working relationships, team dynamics, collaboration, and, consequently, the networks of relationships outside of work.

Though it is difficult to quantify precisely, it is clear that harassment exacts an unacceptable toll on the health and well-being of workers, productivity and social cohesion. The psychosocial and economic costs of workplace psychological harassment add up to an obvious imperative to act. But who can act to stop harassment? The following two chapters consider this question and the parties involved in the complex constellation of relationships in workplace psychological harassment.

Selected references

Andrea, A., & Crawford, N. (1992). *Bullying at work: How to confront and overcome it*. Virago.

Ashforth, B. E. (1997). Petty tyranny in organizations: A preliminary examination of antecedents and consequences. *Canadian Journal of Administrative Sciences/Revue Canadienne des Sciences de l'Administration, 14*(2), 126-140.

Brodsky, C. M. (1976). *The Harassed Worker*. DC Heath & Co.

Duffy, M. K., Ganster, D. C., & Pagon, M. (2002). Social undermining in the workplace. *Academy of management Journal, 45*(2), 331-351.

Einarsen, S and Skogstad, A (1996). Epidemiological findings of bullying. 5(2) *European Work and Organizational Psychologist*, 185–201.

Einarsen, S. V., Hoel, H., Zapf, D., & Cooper, C. L. (Eds.). (2020). *Bullying and harassment in the workplace: Theory, research and practice*. CRC press.

Escartín, J., Ceja, L., Navarro, J., & Zapf, D. (2013). Modeling workplace bullying behaviors using catastrophe theory. *Nonlinear dynamics, psychology, and life sciences, 17*(4), 493-515.

Farrell & Geist-Martin (2005). The Project for Wellness and Work-Life at Arizona State University reports

Farrelly, C., & Solum, L. (Eds.). (2019). *Virtue jurisprudence*. Springer.

Freyd, J., & Birrell, P. (2013). *Blind to betrayal: Why we fool ourselves we aren't being fooled*. Turner Publishing Company.

Freyd, J.J. (1997). Violations of power, adaptive blindness, and betrayal trauma theory. *Feminism & Psychology*, 7, 22-32.

Gewirtz, P. (1995). On I know it when I see it. *Yale LJ, 105*, 1023.

Haslam, C., Jetten, J., Cruwys, T., Dingle, G., & Haslam, S. A. (2018). *The new psychology of health: Unlocking the social cure*. Routledge.

Henderson Jr, J. A. (1975). Expanding the negligence concept: Retreat from the rule of law. *Ind. Lj*, 51, 467.

Hill, J. (2020). *See what you made me do: Power, control and domestic abuse*. Black Inc.

Hutchinson, M. (2013). Bullying as workgroup manipulation: A model for understanding patterns of victimization and contagion within the workgroup. *Journal of nursing management, 21*(3), 563-571.

Jacobellis v. Ohio 378 U.S. 184, 197 (1964) (Stewart, J., concurring).

Keashly, L., & Harvey, S. (2006). Workplace Emotional Abuse. In E. K. Kelloway, J. Barling, & J. J. Hurrell, Jr., *Handbook of workplace violence* (pp. 95–120). Sage.

Leymann, H. (1990). Mobbing and psychological terror at workplaces. *Violence and victims, 5*(2), 119-126.

Leymann, Heinz (1990). *Manual of the LIPT questionnaire for assessing the risk of psychological violence at work*. Stockholm: Violen.

Lutgen-Sandvik, P., Namie, G., & Namie, R. (2010). Workplace bullying: Causes, consequences, and corrections. *Destructive organizational communication*, 43-68.

Maté, G. (2022). *The myth of normal: Trauma, illness, and healing in a toxic culture*. Ebury.

Matyók, T. and Schmitz, C.L. (2010). A story to tell: Bullying and mobbing in the workplace. *International Journal of Business and Social Science, 1*(3), 87-97.

Moayed, F. A., Daraiseh, N., Shell, R., & Salem, S. (2006). Workplace bullying: a systematic review of risk factors and outcomes. *Theoretical Issues in Ergonomics Science, 7*(3), 311-327.

Pauline Rennie Peyton (2003). *Dignity at work: eliminate bullying and create a positive work environment*. Routledge.

Poilpot-Rocaboy, G. (2010). Understanding Workplace Violence: The Case of Psychological Harassment. *Humanisme et Entreprise, 296*(1), 9-24.

Richman, J. A., Flaherty, J. A., & Rospenda, K. M. (1996). Perceived workplace harassment experiences and problem drinking among physicians: Broadening the stress/alienation paradigm. *Addiction, 91*(3), 391-403.

Rosander, M., & Blomberg, S. (2019). Levels of workplace bullying and escalation–a new conceptual model based on cut-off scores, frequency and self-labelled victimization. *European Journal of Work and Organizational Psychology, 28*(6), 769-783.

Sloan, L. M., Matyok, T., Schmitz, C. L., & Short, G. F. L. (2010). A story to tell: Bullying and mobbing in the workplace. *International Journal of Business and Social Science, 1*(3).

Staub, E. (2003). *The psychology of good and evil: Why children, adults, and groups help and harm others*. Cambridge University Press.

Taris, T. W. (2022). What we need to know about workplace bullying. *Work & Stress, 36*(2), 129-132.

Tepper, B. J. (2000). Consequences of abusive supervision. *Academy of management journal, 43*(2), 178-190.

Verkuil, B., Atasayi, S., & Molendijk, M. L. (2015). Workplace bullying and mental health: a meta-analysis on cross-sectional and longitudinal data. *PloS one, 10*(8), e0135225.

WorkCover Corporation (2004) Workplace Bullying. www.workcover.com/ftp/ documents/aeworkplacebullying.pdf.

Zapf, D., & Gross, C. (2001). Conflict escalation and coping with workplace bullying: A replication and extension. *European journal of work and organizational psychology, 10*(4), 497-522.

http://13.211.129.50/wp-content/uploads/2014/03/TMS-White-Paper-Preventing-and-Managing-Workplace-Bullying.pdf.

https://journals.sagepub.com/doi/full/10.1177/1037969X231174672#fn12-1037969X231174672.

https://www.headsup.org.au/docs/default-source/resources/bl1269-brochure---pwc-roi-analysis.pdf?sfvrsn=6.

https://www.reuters.com/article/us-health-heart-bullying/workplace-bullying-and-violence-tied-to-higher-risk-of-heart-problems-idUSKCN1NO2HV.

https://www.safeworkaustralia.gov.au/system/files/documents/1705/bullying-and-harassment-in-australian-workplaces-australian-workplace-barometer-results.pdf Productivity Commission, 2010.

https://www.smh.com.au/business/workplace/more-than-1-million-paid-out-for-workplace-bullying-20161021-gs827s.html.

Chapter Three

A complex constellation of relationships

Keep away from people who try to belittle your ambitions. Small people always do that, but the really great make you feel that you, too, can become great.

Mark Twain

Chapter Introduction

This chapter introduces the cast of characters impacted by and/or influenced by workplace psychological abuse. This network of relationships includes the people who harass and who are harassed, as well as co-workers and other bystanders. Before we can formulate approaches to curtailing harassment, we must understand these networks and motivations.

Definitions and precise characterisations of perpetrators and targets are elusive. But what can be said is that, here, too, for the most part, 'we know it when we see it'. Though not always, we often recognise perpetrators and targets as the harassment plays out. Some of the defining characteristics of perpetrators and targets are highlighted in the first part of this chapter, with the caveat that these characteristics are not consistent, decisive or exhaustive. Comprehending this prepares us to understand better that context creates the conditions for harassment to thrive, which will be explored in more detail in Chapter Four.

This chapter also introduces the important role played by bystanders. Theirs is the story of not wanting to see, not wanting to know, as they/we turn our backs on targets of abuse and, perversely, even side with the bully, compounding the harm.

Who is a perpetrator

There is no one widely agreed, clearly established specific personality type of perpetrators. Though we can expect important new data and information to inform our understanding in the next few years, the picture at this stage is inconclusive. Studies of patterns of behaviour of perpetrators indicate an extensive range of traits and behaviours that may include:

- A strong need for power and control, to assert dominance over others, to intimidate and manipulate.
- Low honesty and humility scores in the HEXACO personality inventory.
- Lack of morality and tendency toward engagement in unethical behaviour.
- Propensity toward exploitation of others.
- Willingness to reframe and invent information for their own ends.
- Disregard or dismissal of the feelings and needs of their targets, focusing solely on their own desires and goals.
- Feelings of inadequacy, low self-esteem or deep-seated insecurities for which emotionally abusive behaviour may be an attempt to compensate.
- Refusal to take responsibility for actions, deflecting blame onto others, manipulating situations to achieve their desired outcomes, as well as to avoid accountability and escape consequences for their behaviour through tactics such as gaslighting, manipulation of information, or undermining the reputation and credibility of their targets.
- Resistance to changes in the workplace that threaten their perceived power or control, targeting individuals who challenge their authority or question their actions.
- Aggressive behaviours, both overt and covert, such as verbal aggression, physical intimidation, threats, or spreading rumours and gossip; and
- Other exacerbating traits are lack of self-control and self-reflection.

Some research links harassing behaviours with psychopathic tendencies, including Machiavellianism and narcissism. While not an officially recognised diagnostic category or personality disorder, the 'Dark Triad' is a concept in psychological research that is sometimes used as a framework for understanding certain personality traits that may be associated with negative outcomes in social interactions. There is work also in progress to validate a 'Dark Tetrad' concept. The traits of the Dark Tetrad are:

- Machiavellianism - a manipulative and exploitative approach to interpersonal relationships, characterised by cunning and strategic behaviours and willingness to use deceit to advance their interests.

- Narcissism - an inflated sense of self-importance, a need for admiration and attention, a lack of empathy for others, an excessive sense of entitlement, prioritising their own needs and desires and difficulty recognising or valuing the feelings and perspectives of others.

- Psychopathy - a lack of empathy, shallow emotions, a tendency towards impulsive and antisocial behaviour, a lack of remorse or guilt, a disregard for social norms and a reduced capacity for forming genuine emotional connections.

- Sadism - self-affirmation or pleasure derived from cruel, humiliating or aggressive behaviours, including 'everyday sadism' observed in the workplace.

The research indicates that Dark Tetrad traits exist on a spectrum, and not everyone who exhibits these traits engages in harmful or abusive behaviour. However, when these traits are highly pronounced, they can contribute to destructive and exploitative behaviour in interpersonal relationships, including the workplace. The presence of executives with these traits risks creating a toxic work environment that can compromise the quality of products and services, delay the delivery of assignments, prevent the recruitment of talent and increase the risk of inappropriate management practices, fraud and corruption.

While some perpetrators exhibit traits of the Dark Tetrad, the evidence suggests others are just unexceptional people lacking good relationship skills. When ambitious, unexceptional people are insecure about their own worth, they can be disposed to manipulative behaviour. They may act in ways identified as pathological, power-addicted and controlling to make themselves feel superior and powerful. They may learn they can get ahead by treating others badly, putting them down, crowding them out and undermining them. Their success in these behaviour patterns depends on their managers' failure to hold them accountable.

Harassment may occur at any level of an organisation, but in a significant percentage of cases the perpetrators are supervisors or managers. Often, the perpetrator is a great salesperson, adept at ingratiating themselves into the C-suite's favour. People who manipulate and control others may gravitate to management roles, particularly in hierarchical cultures. They can be of high social intelligence and adept at influencing. They focus on gaining the sponsorship and support of higher managers and/or human resources. Such managers can be low in trust, creativity, innovation and collaboration and resentful of others with these qualities. Unfortunately, it can be the case that middle managers do not attain their roles by virtue of their excellence, but by conformity.

> '...commonplace in complexion, and features in manners and invoice... He was obeyed, yet he inspired neither love, nor fear, nor even respect. He inspired uneasiness. That was it! Uneasiness. Not a definite mistrust – just uneasiness – nothing more. You have no idea how effective such a ... faculty can be.'
>
> Joseph Conrad, Heart of Darkness

Research is ongoing on the interplay between individual personality traits and organisational culture in the propensity to engage in emotionally abusive behaviour. For employees burdened with onerous responsibilities and expectations, performance targets, deadlines and KPIs, the pressure can translate to emotionally abusive behaviour as a means of exerting control or addressing perceived performance issues. High performers make average performers feel that they look bad, and high standards tend to increase the level of work expected of others. Average performers may prefer others to keep to the same low standard.

Some people become habituated to harassing behaviours. Stories abound of perpetrators cycling through victims, deriving satisfaction from a sense of power over others, which is only more likely to continue when rewarded by employers. As the behaviour is ignored or rewarded, they are encouraged to continue, and become increasingly confident in exerting dominance through harassing tactics. Some develop attitudes of entitlement or impunity, leading to ever more egregious abusive behaviour without fear of consequences, and so the toxic culture grows.

Power informs many of the meanings that work carries in our culture - the struggle for it, the haves and have-nots of the workplace, who has a voice, who is in favour, and who is not. Whatever the underlying causes and motivations behind their behaviour, perpetrators serve at the pleasure of management. They tend to stay in the organisation and are often supported, rewarded, and even promoted. And so, as it increases their power, this damaging behaviour is encouraged.

In sum, it is not always easy to know perpetrators when we see them. It takes skill and experience to identify weeds in a garden, and many that appear innocuous can take hold and cause damage if an inexperienced or inattentive gardener permits. Weeds crowd out the new growth of preferred species, so removing them is a priority. Unless the organisation attends to the weeds in the workplace, their toxicity crowds out the potential for the best workers to flourish and stifles new growth, creativity and innovation.

What it takes to be a target

Asking whether certain personality traits characterize targets may be a little like asking for the characteristic emotional makeup of victims of any form of violence. Sometimes, people act in ways that attract others' actions; sometimes they are simply in the wrong place at the wrong time. Just as there is no established profile for perpetrators, there is no one clear personality type or set of characteristics that defines targets. Some empirical studies conclude that a victim personality profile does not exist. While there are no conclusive answers, research indicates various factors that may contribute to susceptibility to harassment.

Research indicates targets will likely demonstrate intelligence, confidence, creativity, integrity, accomplishment, loyalty and dedication. They are often productive, more individualistic and creative than compliant, which makes sense - if it were otherwise, there would be little point in harassment.

Performance can be a predictor. Targets are often skilled, competent, and dedicated to their work, conscientious overachievers, and sometimes workaholics devoted to their jobs, which makes them more vulnerable. Their abilities and achievements may trigger jealousy or insecurity in the perpetrator, leading to attempts to undermine or sabotage their success. Perpetrators may exploit their conscientiousness by setting unrealistic expectations, micromanaging, or undermining the target's efforts.

Individuals who are empathetic and caring by nature may be more vulnerable to harassment. Their willingness to understand and accommodate the needs of others may be exploited by perpetrators who take advantage of their kindness.

Targets typically do not sit too low on the pecking order, or there would be little need to harass them. Because harassment is used as a way of signalling power, the target is generally of at least some consequence. To dominate a target perceived as weak does not create the right impression.

One study found targets were likely to be victimized because:

- The target is highly productive, thus recalibrating the status quo
- The target is innovative, hence encouraging the revaluation of long-held practices and/or
- The target calls out unethical behaviour, revealing systemic problems.

The researcher notes that all of these are attributes one might expect ethical organisations to value in workers. However, many organisations do not because targets threaten organisational stasis. Communicating assertively, rejecting norms, and overachieving are also suggested antecedents. Some targets may become branded by the perpetrator as provocative, threatening, and needing to be kept in their place.

At the same time, targets are quite likely to be supportive of colleagues and disinclined to self-promotion. Some research suggests that targets tend to be well-liked, ethical, and known for kindness and generosity. HEXACO testing indicates targets score high on honesty but may be too frank and score lower on agreeableness, perhaps especially by their managers.

Though collaborative, they are less likely to be politically motivated, so they may fail to build alliances and, therefore, lack a strong support system within the workplace, making it more challenging for individuals isolated by harassment to get help and support to address the harassing behaviour.

Other research suggests some targets may attract harassment due to anxiety and depression and/or poorer social skills than other colleagues; they may be people who are less able to cope and tend to avoid conflict by giving in. According to some studies, targets may be non-confrontational, preferring to avoid conflict or assertive responses. Perpetrators may perceive this as an opportunity to exert power and control, as the target may be less likely to retaliate or challenge their behaviour. These targets may be more introverted or shy, preferring to keep to themselves or work independently. Their reserved nature of can make them more susceptible to mistreatment and less likely to seek support or confront the perpetrator.

> *I am by nature very shy, quiet and reserved. The word my friends and family use to describe me is 'gentle'. This is partly the personality I was born with, but I have also had a long history of depression and anxiety affecting me to varying degrees throughout my adult life. I have been dealing with these issues, mostly successfully these days, through strategies I have developed with the help and support of psychologists, counsellors and GPs. These strategies include various CBT (Cognitive Behaviour Therapy) techniques and antidepressant medication.*
>
> Submission 257

Neuroticism has also been shown to correlate with being a target, as people with this trait react more intensely to distressing circumstances, perceive situations as more threatening, feel more hopeless when frustrated and experience associated anger, anxiety, and depression. When what matters is impact, as demonstrated by the Leymann Inventory, the ideal targets are sensitive ones.

Discrimination and prejudice can contribute to harassing behaviour. Marginalized groups face a higher risk of being targeted, as harassment often builds from and reinforces prejudice. Targets are often people who are perceived as different due to factors such as race, gender, age, religion, sexual orientation, or disability. (In these circumstances, some targets may be protected by regulation against discrimination.) Vulnerability to harassment has been found to correlate also with personal differences such as foreign status or sex, gender and campus politics to name a few. Younger workers (under age 25) and older workers (over age 55) are at greater risk of being targets.

In the US the Workplace Bullying Institute identified women, African-Americans, and Latinos as at higher risk. The European Foundation identified women as at 75% greater risk of being targets. SafeWork Australia reports that claims for harassment and/or bullying made by female employees were more than twice as high as the rate of these claims made by males over the three years 2015–16 to 2017–18 combined. Similarly, the rates for claims made by females relating to work pressure and exposure to workplace or occupational violence were more than twice that of similar claims made by males. Contributing factors include women's subordination to men in the workplace and concomitantly lower levels of comfort within the cultures of male-dominant workplaces.

Tempting though it would be to try, it is beyond the scope of this book to address the myriad of topics that these paragraphs imply concerning diversity in the workplace. I can say that in my experience, sexism is still rampant. And sadly, while women at the highest levels position themselves to win awards for supporting other women, in reality they may do anything but.

The research suggests that it can be hard to tell whether the identified traits of targets are vulnerabilities and characteristics caused by, rather than causes of harassment. Neither the research nor anecdotal evidence suggests any one set of characteristics or traits that can accurately predict whether or not a person will be a target of harassment. In future, more conclusive research will contribute to effectively addressing relationship dynamics of harassment. What we do know is that the current research emphasises that being a target of harassment is not the fault of the target. A target is anyone in the wrong place at the wrong time who is vulnerable enough to serve the purposes and susceptible to the offences of the perpetrator.

The enabling silence of bystanders

'In the end, we will remember not the words of our enemies, but the silence of our friends.'
The Rev. Martin Luther King, Jr.

We know it when we see it, but only if we are willing to open our eyes. That willingness takes intention, courage and commitment. If workplace psychological harassment is an epidemic, it is because so many choose not to see it, choose to allow it to continue, and fail to demonstrate the intention, courage and commitment to recognise the problem and take real action to fix it.

The 'bystander effect' is a psychological phenomenon where the presence of others discourages a person from intervening - the greater the number of bystanders, the less likely any of them will help. Colleagues have a front-row seat to harassment, and yet so often, they turn a blind eye, leaving targets baffled as to why co-workers systematically fail to respond effectively, people they thought they could rely on and trust

I don't know what turn my life would've taken if people didn't believe me when I said that something had happened to me.
Taylor Swift

There are many reasons why bystanders may choose not to get involved. First, there's the classic, perhaps the simplest explanation – 'not our problem'. Why sign up for it? And besides…They've seen it before. They know complaints do not solve anything. Speaking up will not help and may make things worse.

Colleagues see the writing on the wall and back the winning team. Siding with the target is rarely a winning strategy. Risk-averse bystanders do not want to draw attention to themselves. They fear retribution or becoming another victim. Maybe they've been bullied before and do not want to be bullied again. They think, 'Better the devil you know. At least I'm safe for the moment. We could end up with someone worse who targets me!'

Studies of stigma by association (SBA) in the harassment context indicate that anticipated SBA leads to less helping intentions. Perhaps some co-workers and/or bystanders even believe the target 'deserves' it. Confirmation bias is the tendency to believe the best version of events, in this case, that harassment is not happening. Or if they do believe it, they do not want to become involved. And definitely not on the side that's sure to lose. The bystander should put their head down, keep quiet and focus on work.

Group cohesiveness is the desire for group unity that renders bystanders disinclined to 'rock the boat'. People want and need to keep their jobs. Some bystanders are aligned with the perpetrator, often a person of influence, who may be a friend and/or perceived as a necessary ally. Bystanders may be under pressure themselves; they may be on probation or a casual whose tenure is vulnerable or on a conditional visa or feel some other harassing pressure.

Bystanders have pressures in their lives outside of work as well, and may feel they cannot take this one on. They may not know what to do, so doing nothing is easier. Just go along, be quiet. Pretend that everything is fine. That's what we want to believe anyway. The organisation does not want problems, so processes discourage speaking up. No wonder bystanders do nothing. It is so much easier. And that's all the perpetrator asks.

Common reactions to seeing their colleagues being mistreated:

- *stand idly by and not assist the targets.*
- *turn on targets by avoiding and isolating them, not sharing critical information with them, spreading gossip about them (often presented as 'concern'), blaming them, denying previous supportive statements made to them, denying what they have witnessed, and aligning with perpetrators.*

The main cause of the first reaction is the 'diffusion of responsibility' phenomenon, that is, the more observers there are, the less likely observers are willing to assist the target because of the expectation that someone else will help or that it is someone else's responsibility to help. The main cause of the second reaction is a fear that job security/career advancement can be jeopardised or there is risk of being victimised by being associated with, or supportive of, an employee who has fallen out of favour.

Submission 252

Often, bystanders put as much distance as possible between themselves and the target. 'The victim demands action, engagement and remembering.' The target asks the bystander to risk becoming a victim with them. So, to protect themselves, workers do what management wants; they pretend not to see. They become skilled in the dark arts of surviving a toxic workplace, hunkering down and looking after their own self-interest, being wary and mistrustful, and not sharing information. At the same time, the organisation espouses values of teamwork, collaboration and healthy workplace culture.

> *We all have some knowledge of what's going on. Doing nothing is a decision.*
> Personal diary

Sometimes, it is more than passive turning away. Mobbing happens when bystanders are recruited into the abuse. So, it is not just the perpetrator, as others can and do compound the harm exponentially. Recruiting bystanders into the abuse adds to the betrayal, compounds the harm, and makes any possibility of resolution that much more elusive.

> *Unfortunately, the colleague (my replacement) I confided in was a co-conspirator which resulted in a double betrayal.*
> Submission 290

To do nothing is, essentially, to side with the perpetrator. Moral disengagement equates to managerial and bystander support of the process of violence, but it comes at a cost. Bystanders who do not intervene or report harassment often suffer negative consequences themselves. They may experience pressure to participate in the harassment, anxiety about speaking to anyone about the harassment, powerlessness to stop harassment, vulnerability to becoming victimized, fear of associating with the target, the perpetrator, or the perpetrator's pals, and guilt for not having defended or supported the target.

> *The bullying ...is septic. This fellow has a few 'chosen ones' and they are encouraged to use the same bullying tactics.*
> Submission 37

In toxic work environments, each staff member develops their own particular strategy for survival. In addition to deliberate 'not-knowing', other strategies include watching your back, not trusting anyone, and keeping to yourself. Complaining is an unpleasant process and feels very negative. It's also time-consuming; people want to be positive and do good things. Perhaps most importantly, the common (sadly, accurate) view is that complaints rarely lead to remedial action, and do often lead to recrimination. It becomes an insidious reinforcement to a harassing manager's control. Staff are afraid, and realise that speaking up runs counter to their interests and often their own natures and values of safety, cooperation and belonging.

Chapter conclusion

There is no one widely agreed, clearly established, specific personality type we can use to identify or predict a person who harasses others. We know their toxicity crowds out the potential for the best workers to flourish.

There is no one widely agreed, clearly established specific personality type of targets. What we do know is that to be a targets is to be a signal species of the danger to worker safety. A target is anyone in the wrong place at the wrong time who is vulnerable enough to serve the purpose and susceptible to the offences of the perpetrator.

The role of bystanders is critical. They provide solidarity, support, and witnessing. And yet, bystanders choose not to get involved for many reasons. The silence is enabling; it prevents progress toward a safe workplace, but it will continue as long as it is not safe to speak.

As long as it is unsafe to support targets, targets will not be supported. One way to counter this dynamic is to make supporting targets safe and encouraged through awareness, solidarity and good leadership. For this, we look at the organisation's context and management's role, discussed in the next chapter.

Selected references

Adams, A. (1992). *Bullying at work: How to confront and overcome it*, Virago, London.

Baughman, H. M., Dearing, S., Giammarco, E., & Vernon, P. A. (2012). Relationships between bullying behaviours and the Dark Triad: A study with adults. *Personality and Individual Differences, 52*(5), 571-575.

Bokek-Cohen, Y. A., Shkoler, O., & Meiri, E. (2023). The unique practices of workplace bullying in academe: An exploratory study. *Current Psychology, 42*(23), 19466-19485.

Coyne, I., Seigne I. & Randall, P. (2000). Predicting workplace victim status from personality, *European Journal of Work and Organisational Psychology,* 9:3, 335-349.

Dåderman, A. M., & Ragnestål-Impola, C. (2019). Workplace bullies, not their victims, score high on the Dark Triad and extraversion, and low on agreeableness and honesty-humility. *Heliyon, 5*(10).

Davenport, T. H., Thomas, R. J., & Cantrell, S. (2002). The mysterious art and science of knowledge-worker performance. *MIT Sloan Management Review*.

Einarsen, S. (1999). The nature and causes of bullying at work. *International journal of manpower, 20*(1/2), 16-27.

Field, T. (1996). *Bully in sight: How to predict, resist, challenge and combat workplace bullying: Overcoming the silence and denial by which abuse thrives*. Success Unlimited.

Glasø, L., Stig B., Morten, B.N .and Einarsen, S. (2007). Do targets of workplace bullying portray a general victim personality profile?. *Scandinavian journal of psychology 48*, no. 4.

Góis, A. D., Lima, G. A. S. F. D., & De Luca, M. M. M. (2020). Everyday sadism in the business area. *RAUSP Management Journal, 55*, 393-408.

Herman, J. L. (2015). *Trauma and recovery: The aftermath of violence-- from domestic abuse to political terror*. Hachette UK.

HEXACO personality inventory at https://hexaco.org/scaledescriptions.

Hodgins, M. (2021). Taking on the institution: An autoethnographic account. *Societies, 11*(2), 39.

Huesmann, L. R., Eron, L. D., Lefkowitz, M. M., & Walder, L. O. (1984). Stability of aggression over time and generations. *Developmental Psychology, 20*: 1120–1134.

Lutgen-Sandvik, P., Namie, G., & Namie, R. (2010). Workplace bullying: Causes, consequences, and corrections. *Destructive organizational communication*, 43-68.

Matthiesen, S. B., & Einarsen, S. (2001). MMPI-2 configurations among victims of bullying at work. *European Journal of Work and Organizational Psychology, 10*(4), 467-484.

Matyók, T. and Schmitz, C.L. (2010). A story to tell: Bullying and mobbing in the workplace. *International Journal of Business and Social Science, 1*(3), 87-97.

Mulder, R., Pouwelse, M., Lodewijkx, H., & Bolman, C. (2014). Workplace mobbing and bystanders' helping behaviour towards victims: The role of gender, perceived responsibility and anticipated stigma by association. *International Journal of Psychology, 49*(4), 304-312.

Namie, G., & Namie, R. (2009). US Workplace bullying: Some basic considerations and consultation interventions. *Consulting Psychology Journal: Practice and Research, 61*(3), 202.

D. L. & Williams, K. (2002). The Dark Triad of personality: Narcissism, machiavellianism, and psychopathy. *Journal of Research in Personality, 36:* 556-568.

Pilch, I., & Turska, E. (2015). Relationships between Machiavellianism, organizational culture, and workplace bullying: Emotional abuse from the target's and the perpetrator's perspective. *Journal of Business Ethics, 128*, 83-93.

Thornberg, R., & Jungert, T. (2013). Bystander behavior in bullying situations: Basic moral sensitivity, moral disengagement and defender self-efficacy. *Journal of Adolescence*, 36(3), 475-483.

Volk Developmental Science Lab, Brock University, Ontario, Canada.

https://www.safetydimensions.com.au/industries-with-highest-frequency-rates-of-work-related-harassment-bullying/.

Chapter Four

Cultures of silence at work

In teamwork, silence isn't golden, it's deadly.
Mark Sanborn

Chapter Introduction

This chapter explores the crucial role of organizational factors as causes of harassment and the motivations of management in minimising the issue, not only permitting but encouraging it to persist. The chapter describes the opportunistic instrumentalism of the perpetrator, where the answer to the question, 'Why do abusers abuse?' is simply and tragically, 'Because they can.' In the domestic abuse context there are programs to help people who abuse change these patterns of behaviour. Similar work can be done in the workplace context, to change abusive patterns of behaviour at work, at the individual and systems levels.

But there are important barriers to action. In this Chapter we begin to see how psychological abuse among workers can, in perverse ways, reinforce management self-interest and control. This phenomenon helps explain management's systematic failure to recognise the problem, respond to and remediate it, along with tactics to deny and minimise it. Effectively, management remains not only untainted, but indeed can be empowered by the bad behaviour of employees. Especially in contexts where their accountability is otherwise elusive and or confused, management is heavily focussed on protecting their own power, and so has little motivation to stop psychological harassment.

Organisational factors that cause harassment

Psychosocial climate, management styles, working conditions

After many years studying the subject, researcher Michelle Tuckey observed, 'I've come to understand ...bullying is not the disease. Rather, it's a *symptom* of poor organisational functioning; organisational factors rather than individual personality traits are the main potential causes.' Tuckey's view is supported by meta-analytic evidence from nearly 100 studies indicating that organisation-level factors are the fundamental determinants of bullying. Harassment thrives in workplaces with dysfunctional work design, leadership practices and organisational culture, such as those characterised by gossip, manipulation, exclusion, and sabotage. Organisational antecedents and triggers shown to correlate positively with harassment include those with:

- **Low psychosocial safety climates, characterised by, e.g.**
  - Work group competition and hostility.
  - Poor workplace relationships.
  - High levels of interpersonal conflict.
  - Abusive and demeaning behaviour, including inappropriate or derogatory language.
  - Pervasive criticism and negative feedback.
- **Lack of behavioural standards and unreasonable expectations, characterised by, e.g.**
  - A culture that accepts and/or even rewards unreasonable workplace behaviours.
  - Perceived or real inequities of resources.
  - Low levels of support.
  - Low moral standards.
  - Isolation.
  - Lack of procedural justice .
- **High-pressure work environments, characterised by, e.g.**

- High job demands with limited control.
- High levels of tension, stress, pressure and/or frustration.
- Poor physical working conditions, including moves to open plan.
- Uncertainty and instability.
- Financially challenged organisations that can least afford the loss of productivity that harassment causes.

- **Authoritarian management styles, characterised by, e.g.**
- Autocratic behaviour that is strict and directive and does not allow workers to take part in decision-making.
- Power imbalances.
- Poor communication processes.
- Environments where employees are fearful of speaking up and voicing opinions.

- **Laissez-faire management styles, characterised by, e.g.**
- Lack of clear work goals.
- Lack of clear performance feedback.
- Frequently changing or ambiguous work situations and unclear duties.
- Lack of systems to deal with conflict.
- A climate of informality—relaxed though such a climate may be—can inadvertently facilitate the spread of incivility through an organisation.

- **High rates of change, characterised by, e.g.**
- Restructuring, significant technological change, role transition and ambiguity, job insecurity.
- Confusion, uncertainty, ambiguity over roles and responsibilities.
- Lack of appropriate training, inappropriate scheduling, poorly designed rostering, and unreasonable performance measures or timeframes.
- Low levels of job autonomy.

- o   Monotonous tasks, rotating tasks.
- o   Unpredictable expectations.
- o   High levels of job insecurity or strain leading to unmet needs.
- **Major precipitating factors or triggers such as restructuring, downsizing, organisational change, characterised by, e.g.**
- o   Merger or acquisition, or reduction in workforce.
- o   Restructuring and competition marginalising groups within the organisation, leading to factionalism.
- o   Mismanagement of change and transition.

<u>Industries/sectors with high rates of harassment</u>

Sectors that register the highest rates of claims for work-related harassment include public order and safety services; residential care services; civic, professional and interest group services; education; hospitals and health care; child care; and government administration. Various explanations are posited for prevalence in certain sectors and settings. A significant factor in this may be that service performance is often intangible, with difficult-to-measure training and KPIs. Though the relational quality lends itself to the possibility of rewarding and fulfilling work, it can also make the workplace more susceptible to relational conflicts. Precise job expectations and performance-based feedback can be challenging to achieve in these work environments. Also, these sectors can be stubbornly hierarchical and highly politicised.

Additionally, government-funded sectors may carry fewer immediate repercussions for harassment costs. Managers *in situ* are often less accountable for losing productivity over the long term or for the costs of stonewalling and protracted legal battles to protect themselves and their cronies. Sadly, this is the opposite of the kind of 'extreme ownership' advocated by many management experts.

> *Unfortunately, I personally know of too many instances where the complainant and/or whistleblower has been destroyed by a culture that promotes and condones workplace bullying. That the University places higher credibility on traits of malevolence, malice, cowardice and self-protection rather than upholding values of excellence and integrity is shameful and should be exposed.*
>
> Submission 8

Though they may be insulated to some degree from the risks of their public sector and not-for-profit counterparts, for-profit corporate environments are susceptible to harassment as well. Their legal structure permits profit-driven corporations to externalize costs and escape accountability for negative social and environmental impacts. The pressure to meet financial targets and maximize shareholder value contributes to decision-making based principally on profit with concomitant deficits of empathy and concern for the welfare of others. This dynamic can be expected to attract and reward individuals who thrive in such an environment. Thus, these organisations' resulting hierarchical structures, profit-driven goals, and legal protections combine to fuel unsafe behavioural practices, including unethical behaviours.

Culture is critical to corporate success. By allowing firms to attract and retain top-performing employees, a healthy, safe workplace culture underpins employee productivity and morale. However, culture cuts both ways; it can also be a determinant of dysfunctional organisations. Given the number of ways that organisational cultures can risk correlating positively with harassment, maintaining a healthy workplace is a big task and a never-ending one. Unhappy workplaces are all unhappy in their own ways. Like all relationships, this is not easy, not set and forget, but it requires regular attention.

Perverse incentives

Workplace psychological harassment is a work culture problem; it can be stopped, and the damage minimised, especially at the early stages, through good management practice and a safe workplace culture. Whatever industry or sector we are talking about, harassment can only persist if management permits, continuing to pay perpetrators to carry on in the positions from which they can abuse, and even promoting them, engraining cultures of harassment at the highest levels.

What, then, can explain why people with the authority and the responsibility to improve organisational culture instead allow cultures conducive to harassment to persist? And why, in many workplaces, do those in authority allow the damage to amplify and the behaviours to escalate instead of taking the opportunity to address the problem and fix the culture? What can explain why management minimises or ignores the issue, rewards the perpetrators and punishes targets?

Harassment thrives when it is preferred to the alternative, which is change. There will be no investment in changing workplace culture as long as the investment that matters most is in the status quo. The truth is that harassment benefits management interests by preserving the status quo that keeps them in control. And their ethos regarding harassment is often characterised by the following three guiding principles – deny, do not respond, and do not validate a whistleblower (even a bad manager is better than a whistleblower).

Management guiding principle number one:

Deny the problem. Speaking up threatens the status quo so carefully crafted by those in power. A very effective way to avoid a problem is to not recognise that it exists.

The fact that research overwhelmingly points to organisational culture as the key cause of harassment is hardly welcome news for managers. They do not want to admit problems exist within the organisation that might tarnish brand capital and their reputations as good leaders. Nor do they want to be accountable for appointing or promoting alleged perpetrators to positions of influence. Acknowledging problems with workplace culture invokes the need to act; something must be done to change it. That sort of work is time-consuming and expensive. It gets in the way of the 'real job', i.e. bottom line results, sales, launching new products, and building a positive brand image. Dealing with complaints is an unwelcome distraction. They do not see much upside in time spent on 'playground duties'. And because they do not themselves feel the harm of the abuse, they fail to see addressing the problem as an urgent matter, as targets do. Though senior management cannot get away with the 'not my problem' excuse as easily as bystanders, they can minimise and deflect the matter as simply a conflict between two individuals, effectively equating to 'not my problem'.

One could be forgiven for imagining that management would regard complaints as opportunities to improve the workplace. But this is often not the case because that would counter their narrative that everything is running perfectly under their excellent leadership. Even if a manager wants to do the right thing, once they ascend to a position of power, keeping their perspective and retaining their values is difficult. People treat them differently as if they have some special status. So, it becomes a shared belief and then a reality, and this quickly becomes dangerous. The morality play of the professional-managerial class espouses values such as integrity, openness, diversity, respect and claiming to take harassment seriously. But if at least one in five workers is harassed, are they really taking it seriously?

Management must be seen as doing the right things, creating a positive workplace culture, and stopping harassment. However, they tend to be more interested in the security of their own positions, power, control, and approval. They are less interested in building safe cultures because of the morality play and the toxic positivity that reinforce their monopoly on virtue. Things cannot be seen going wrong on their watch, as this threatens their security. And, frankly, why would they really want healthy workplaces where employees are empowered? Empowered employees speak up, and speaking up threatens incumbent management's domination and control in the organisation. As the saying goes, for those accustomed to privilege, equality feels like oppression.

Management guiding principle number two:

Nothing to see here. Do not seek solutions. A problem not responded to is not a problem.

At first, it's just confusing; it doesn't make sense to the target experiencing the harm. If management knew a piece of machinery caused harm to workers, they would replace it, right? So why do they not fix the problem when a person harms other workers? Not only do they not fix it, but very often, they do the opposite, putting their support behind the perpetrator. They leave the harmed worker to fend for themselves, or worse, turn against the target, compounding the harm. This institutional betrayal can be one of the most damaging aspects of the experience, not just for targets but more widely, as it perpetuates toxic work conditions throughout the workplace.

If an issue of harassment arises that cannot be ignored (and only a very few fall into that category), organisations can still minimise the matter. They will also point to the practical challenges of addressing it, for example, around proof and evidence and the difficulty of establishing the causation of psychological harm. These practical challenges can be addressed successfully if there is the motivation to do so. However, because it suits employers that the process is ineffective, they prefer to categorise reports of harassment as non-issues, whether by subtle or not-so-subtle means. A classic example is the story of a task force set up in one workplace in response to a growing reputation for an unhealthy culture. When the task force was inundated with reports, management decided to disband it, rather than deal with all the complaints. No task force, no complaints, no problem.

The 'no problem' approach relieves management of the obligation to spend time, money or energy in response. And even if there is a problem, it's not a major problem; it's just a 'minor personal disagreement' or a conflict between two people, so it's not *our* problem to resolve.

HR/P&C can be uncooperative, slow and inefficient because they are under no pressure from senior management to handle complaints effectively—quite the opposite. By handling complaints ineffectively, dragging the process out for months and years, and making it opaque, frustrating and/or difficult for targets, organisations achieve the desired end – workers will not report because they know the complaints process is costly and futile, and may end up harming them. Silence is enforced passively-aggressively. No problem.

Management guiding principle number three:

Even a bad manager is better than a whistleblower.

Good employees do not indulge in the excesses of saying what they think. They don't complain. This ethos underpins the current phenomenon of toxic positivity in the workplace. The employee who speaks about harassment in the workplace threatens the status quo, incumbent power structures and reputational capital. No wonder management and HR/P&C support the perpetrator. In management's view, even a bad manager is better than a whistleblower.

When a target chooses voice, they believe they are acting as a loyal employee in the best interests of the organisation. They want to stay with the organisation but under safe conditions. Unaware of management's guiding principles, they believe that the employer is interested in reducing harassment and will support them in standing up to try to stop it. But what commonly happens is the last thing they expect – they are met with employer betrayal.

In the eyes of management, the target who reports has a newly earned and unsavoury status as a whistleblower and is now a disloyal employee. As they see it, the target has betrayed the employer. The target is 'not one of us', 'doesn't understand how the game is played'. In hierarchical structures, these are cardinal sins.

Management is about power; power is about control, and control belongs to them. Workers should know their place – and be seen to know it. Those who do not are 'not in the tent' probably never will be. The target has shown their colours as a whistleblower. To what, and to whom will they point to next? Better they should go.

> [M]ost targets of bullying do not believe that they deserved the bullying and are shocked when they discover what has been occurring. They are confused and then appalled when their employer, who assured them of safety and respectful conflict resolution practices, turns against them and makes everything worse, eventually forcing them out.
>
> Submission 58

Because speaking up is unwelcome, management harbours a reflexive antagonism toward reporting. Remember the kid who cried, 'I'll tell the teacher!'? Who liked that person? But unlike teachers, who usually have little sympathy with the schoolyard bully, management interests often do align with the perpetrator of harassment for any combination of reasons that may include:

- In-group bias, solidarity with colleagues in close association, even those who behave badly. Perpetrators can be colleagues senior management protects, 'one of us' in management's eyes, and almost always more 'one of us' than the target. The effects may be particularly insidious and infectious to the wider social sphere in settings such as the public service, education and health care systems.

- Management is more likely to be populated with personalities aligned with the perpetrator's power and abusive and coercively controlling behaviours, particularly in hierarchical, individualistic, managerial organisations. Research is ongoing on the interplay between individual personality traits and organisational culture.

- Some people spend years honing their skills in the perversities of office politics to work their way into the C-suite and gain their place at court, so to speak, in the higher echelons of power. This is what is most important to them. They won't easily give up their hard earned rank for the sake of one personal relationship or friendship.

- Special knowledge, skills and/or relationships valuable to the organisation may be attributed to the perpetrator, giving the organisation reason to overlook and/or cover up their misconduct.
- Claims and beliefs that the perpetrator is an effective manager, who, according to their own narrative, is 'just trying to do their job' and 'it's so hard these days...' and 'my staff is so difficult', leading senior managers to sympathise and feel solidarity.
- For the organisational morality play of internal 'discipline', management actually needs their 'bad boys' (and girls) – whose occasional, minor bad behaviour (and that's all it is, right?) enhances management levers of control. It keeps the rank and file on their toes; workers jockeying for positions are easier to keep in line. A bit of tough management (and that's all it is, right? tough, but reasonable) can be a good thing.
- Incompetence can be a characteristic of people in leadership roles because the choice of leaders is often based on confidence, even if misplaced, and charisma, with like attracting like, exacerbating the problem.
- Management supports the perpetrator because a chink in the armour of the perpetrator contributes to the strength and credence of the target; this must be avoided at all costs. Management is antagonistic not only toward complaints in general but toward complainants. Complaining is insubordination, challenging the status quo that management, in their wisdom, has put in place. It is for management to decide who stays and who goes; unsolicited input from the rank and file is anything but welcome.

Senior management may not know what's going on, or not infrequently, they have lost touch, and so their genuine empathy and concern are diminished. But the fact is their duty to know and to act. It is not enough to say the right things. Managers may see maintaining the status quo, which includes protecting a perpetrator, as a short-term saving. However, the fact is that in the long-term, harassment is more costly, though often in ways that aren't measured and carry no accountability. It may seem easier and more expedient to focus on precise measurable performance metrics and short-term financial results rather than the organisation's long-term health. However, the organisation's long-term health matters as much or more than short-term results.

Management escapes accountability for the organisation's culture, including the bad behaviour of their reports, and yet we wonder why things continue as they are. Sadly, many in management secure their positions for reasons less salutary than demonstrated capability as leaders. Tomas Chamorro-Premuzic of University College London, Columbia, and Harvard observes that good leadership is the exception, not the norm. His research indicates that leaders are chosen for traits incompatible with effective leadership, such as overconfidence and narcissism. This results in 'a pathological system' that rewards incompetence and punishes incompetence, to everybody's detriment. How long will we continue to tolerate what author Gideon Haigh calls 'the mundanity of mismanagement' when it costs us so dearly?

It is not an accident that management in hierarchical structures closes ranks with perpetrators. But where it is inadvertent, that is not an excuse. Whatever characteristics may be found among targets and perpetrators, harassment is a relational dynamic that is either supported or thwarted by the system, the workplace culture and environment, the time, the place, the context and the 'leaders' who support perpetrators (even when they say they don't).

Strategies and tactics for maintaining the silence

The one who makes the rules wins the game
Molly Bloom

There is a good deal at stake here. To effect change means asking for nothing less than a shift around *who sets the rules*. Management defines what is and is not acceptable workplace behaviour, including what is and is not legitimate management technique. But, as discussed in Chapter Two, what workplace psychological harassment is (and is not) really needs to be what the collective agrees to at a given place and time. It is for all of us to be informed, aware and mutually protected.

Defining what is and is not acceptable workplace behaviour should not be a captain's call. To begin to turn the tide on psychological harassment requires a collective conversation about what is and is not acceptable and community standards that are widely understood and adhered to rather than *ad hoc* rules set by the few who live above them.

Such a shift, however, threatens managerial power. To inoculate themselves against the taint of uncivil behaviour, reinforce their moral superiority, and retain their monopoly on rule-making, they trumpet diversity, equity, inclusivity and belonging. They insist on 'right language', *saying* what is considered morally correct while neglecting the *practice* of equity in genuinely inclusive and nuanced ways that nurture diversity beyond the labels.

What's most striking at the bottom of all this is that the we-vs-they dynamic itself serves management. It is good to keep workers uncomfortable because workers' enmity serves them. Without it why would we need them?

Tactics to deny, minimise and shift accountability

The watchwords are fail-safe positivity, deference, not-our-problem and the non-issue imperative. One must not see anything because there is nothing to see. One must not speak up about anything except to praise management. To respond to the issue in any genuine or effective way is to be avoided because to respond is to recognise. To deny and deflect harassment issues and obviate the need for response and remediation, an employer has a range of tactics at its disposal. Three in particular, the dyadic dodge, DARVO and outrage management, are discussed in more detail below.

Psychological harassment passed off as garden-variety conflict, aka the 'dyadic dodge'

All cultures and institutions have underlying belief systems supported by stories and myths. The dyadic dodge builds upon the myth that harassment is just a conflict between two people. This myth serves management in several ways, strengthening its power at the expense of both the perpetrator and the target. The reality is that harassment is not conflict; it is abuse. And it is not simply about the interaction between two people; as we have seen, it is the organisational context that creates the conditions for harassment to thrive. Harassment is distinct from mutual conflict in terms of power and intent.

Psychological harassment is not the same as two people of equal status having personal differences. When parties can equally defend themselves, the situation may be a serious conflict, but it is not harassment. Harassment can and often does arise without any real conflict between the actor and the target. It is predatory; the perpetrator intends to destabilise the target and is not interested in conflict resolution processes. Instead, they will game the process to damage the target further and ingratiate themselves with their managers.

Though research consistently points to organisational culture as the key underlying cause of harassment, the myth of dyadic conflict allows employers to keep the focus and accountability on targets and perpetrators, disempowering both and reinforcing management power and control. Perpetuating the myth that workplace psychological harassment is simply a conflict between two parties misrepresents the nature of the problem. It is similar to 'person-blaming' individuals for social problems, assigning blame to individuals for what research has shown is predominantly an organisational problem.

This myth absolves the organisation while reinforcing stereotypes, making it harder to implement change. This is not to say that the individuals involved don't play a role; of course they do. But this framing skews the matter in a way that obstructs genuine resolution. By framing the target as the problem in this dyadic conflict, the one that needs to go, the employer reinforces the support for the behaviours of the perpetrator who remains in their position or is promoted under the thumb of the indulgent overseer, thus strengthening the power of management.

If the target were to prevail, that would challenge existing power structures, which is contrary to management interests. Instead, framing the target as the source of the problem creates an implicit understanding that when the target leaves or is silenced, the problem-that-never-was will disappear. Everyone can breathe a sigh of relief; the storm has passed until it starts over with the next target and the next. A complaint that is unresolved, denied, or ignored is not 'not a problem'. It becomes a bigger problem.

There are additional interesting dimensions of framing abuse of power as conflict in this context that further destabilise a target. One is that these dynamics occur with greater frequency where there is a pre-existing power imbalance. Framing the matter as a conflict between equals tends to vitiate this significant factor. Another dimension is the social value of the sanctity of privacy. In the privacy of interpersonal conflict, the target can be blamed for failing to respect this privacy while complaining to others, such as HR/P&C or more senior managers. The target is the tattle-tale who doesn't respect boundaries and can't deal effectively with their own problems.

To summarise, dyadic framing of harassment absolves the organisation of accountability, and it avoids engagement with the problem of harassment through a transformative process consistent with the values of collaborative teams, mutual support, and a culture of inclusivity. It keeps both the perpetrator and the target in line, subordinating both in postures of deference. It also signals bystanders that it is better to stay out of it, as well as providing a compelling demonstration of the pitfalls of filing complaints. Deflection is done with such conviction that it can only serve to encourage the behaviours and unhealthy culture to thrive.

Institutional DARVO

Employer betrayal may be much more than failure to support the target or to effectively respond to the problem of reported harassment. Deny, Attack, and Reverse Victim and Offender (DARVO) is an effective tactic the perpetrator uses to shift the blame and make the target the problem. Targets are often horrified to discover that the same tactic is carried out by the organisation or with its complicity, impacting in ways that can be worse than the original harassment.

> *I wish to draw to your attention: the entrenched systematic culture of bullying at the University; the lack of support from the University following my initial allegation of bullying; and more importantly the enforced punitive punishment regime I experienced following my submission of a formal grievance that attempted to expose bullying within the workplace....In reflection, the bullying that I experienced within my discipline was nothing compared to the institutionalised bullying that I experienced from university senior management following the submission of my formal grievance. For over three years, I lived in a Kafkaesque-Orwellian nightmare where the truth no longer existed, and lies were accepted as truth. The stress that I suffered*

resulted in the breakup of my marriage, and my forced early retirement has created personal financial difficulties.

Submission 8

Researchers point to this phenomenon with different descriptions, but the common theme is the realisation that the target will not be supported and that the entire organisation is turned against them. Matthew Sharpe calls this the 'one-two punch', and Leymann asserts that the real harm occurs at this point, when the target makes this realisation that there will be no help, rather than the reverse.

The realisation that the organisation would do nothing – even worse, that it would make me the wrongdoer in all this – totally undermined my belief system, my values. And led to retirement many years before I had intended, with major financial consequences. The way the institution responded was far worse than the original crude undermining of the bully. I wonder now how I could ever have believed organisations and management really did want to stop workplace harassment...

Personal diary

Outrage management

Outrage management involves a range of strategies to minimise an issue in circumstances where disclosure of an offending act causes public outcry. Outrage management aims to undermine the outcry and avoid accountability. Applied in the context of harassment, it is about ensuring that the matter is minimised and the target is kept in a losing position. Outrage management tactics include:

1. Covering up or denying the harassment, or simply behaving as if nothing happened.

2. Devaluing the target, portraying them as inferior, paranoid, lazy, unstable, complaining, devious, etc so that the mistreatment does not seem as bad.

3. Reinterpreting the behaviour by lying, minimising, blaming, giving a different explanation for the mistreatment that makes it seem more acceptable, or reframing the harassing behaviour as actually supportive, well-intentioned, justified and legitimate.

4. Using official channels to give an appearance of justice, such as advising workers to put in a formal complaint, use a grievance procedure or even go to court, when these processes seldom

lead to a satisfactory outcome, and not infrequently become a new avenue of harassment and humiliation.

5. Intimidating or bribing targets or witnesses so they fear an escalation of harassment, dismissal or legal action should they do anything about it.

Now that I have left, the world is beginning to look once again like a place that can be happy. I'm sorry I ever got into that organisation. I'm sorry I ever believed that they said they wanted things to be different. I wish they just told me this is how we are and we want to be 'Yes, Minister'; we want to be those people in 'Utopia'. That's who we are. We like things this way and we don't want to change even though we say we do. But of course, they can't say that because that would be honest, and that's not very 'Yes, Minister'...

Personal diary

All three tactics - the dyadic dodge, DARVO and outrage management – deny, minimise and/or shift accountability. They are part of the complaints process charade. Together with stigmatisation and devaluation, these tactics advance the process of pushing the target out. Canaries in coal mines fall off the perch. Fortunately, most of the time, targets do not succumb so spectacularly. But they become buried with forms and requirements, punished with stigma and isolation, frustrated with inaction and ineffective process, all under the pretence that there is nothing wrong until, sooner or later, they go away.

Chapter conclusion

The weight of research points to organisational factors as the principal causes of workplace psychological harassment. Yet one study showed that nearly half the workers who reported instances of harassment perceived that the organisation did nothing in response. About 18% perceived that the harassment behaviours worsened after the report was made, and 40% left the organisation with no harassment reports lodged and, therefore, no action taken to address the behaviour. The three principles of management - that good employees don't complain; a problem not recognised or responded to is not a problem; and even a bad manager is better than a whistleblower - in practice means there must be no speaking up; there must be no real recognition, there can be no effective response. The employer uses the dyadic dodge, DARVO and outrage management tactics to simultaneously deny, minimise and distance itself from the problem. Management's guiding principles and tactics ensure that the target will be silenced and that management itself will emerge untainted, with the perpetrator in its debt and the culture of silence further reinforced.

Selected references

Andersson, L. M., & Pearson, C. M. (1999). Tit for tat? The spiraling effect of incivility in the workplace. *Academy of management review*, 24(3), 452-471.

Baillien, E., Escartín, J., Gross, C., & Zapf, D. (2017). Towards a conceptual and empirical differentiation between workplace bullying and interpersonal conflict. *European Journal of Work and Organizational Psychology, 26*(6), 870-881.

Bakan, J. (2012). *The corporation: The pathological pursuit of profit and power*. Hachette UK.

Chamorro-Premuzic, T. (2019). *Why do so many incompetent men become leaders?: (And how to fix it)*. Harvard Business Press.

Einarsen, S. (1999). The nature and causes of bullying at work. *International Journal of Manpower, 20*(1/2), 16-27.

Feijó, F. R., Gräf, D. D., Pearce, N., & Fassa, A. G. (2019). Risk factors for workplace bullying: a systematic review. *International journal of environmental research and public health, 16*(11), 1945.

Freyd, J.J. (1997). Violations of power, adaptive blindness, and betrayal trauma theory. *Feminism & Psychology, 7*, 22-32.

Haigh, G. (2004). *Bad company: The strange cult of the CEO*. White Lion Publishing.

Martin, B. (2007). 'Tactics against bullying at work' https://www.bmartin.cc/pubs/07bullying.html (and backfire materials at https://www.bmartin.cc/pubs/backfire.html).

Leymann, H. (1990). *Mobbing and psychological terror at workplaces. Violence and victims, 5*(2), 119-126.

Liu, C. (2021). *Virtue hoarders: The case against the professional managerial class*. University of Minnesota Press.

Lutgen-Sandvik, P., Namie, G., & Namie, R. (2010). Workplace bullying: Causes, consequences, and corrections. *Destructive organizational communication*, 43-68.

Nielsen, M. B., & Einarsen, S. (2012). Outcomes of exposure to workplace bullying: A meta-analytic review. *Work & Stress, 26*(4), 309-332.

Potter, R. E., Dollard, M., & Tuckey, M. R. (2016). *Bullying and harassment in Australian workplaces: results from the Australian workplace barometer 2014/15*. Safe Work Australia, University of South Australia.

Sadri, G., & Lees, B. (2001). Developing corporate culture as a competitive advantage. *Journal of management Development, 20*(10), 853-859.

Sharpe, M. (2022). *Stoicism, bullying and beyond: How to keep your head when others around you are losing theirs and blame you*, Balboa Press.

Tee, S., Özçetin, Y. S. Ü., & Russell-Westhead, M. (2016). Workplace violence experienced by nursing students: A UK survey. *Nurse education today, 41*, 30-35.

http://13.211.129.50/wp-content/uploads/2014/03/TMS-White-Paper-Preventing-and-Managing-Workplace-Bullying.pdf.

https://theconversation.com/like-a-cancer-of-the-workplace-bullying-is-a-symptom-of-dysfunction-43831.

https://www.safeworkaustralia.gov.au/sites/default/files/2021-06/D21%209238%20Psychosocial_health_and_safety_and_bullying_in_australian_workplaces_6th_edition.pdf.

Chapter Five

The secret rules

Each time a man stands up for an ideal, or acts to improve the lot of others, or strikes out against injustice, he sends forth a tiny ripple of hope.
Robert F. Kennedy

Chapter Introduction

Targets try to 'play nice', thinking they can still be regarded as 'good employees'. In the meantime, management, and their henchmen, HR/People and Culture (HR/P&C), play by secret rules that targets aren't supposed to know. But they need to know. Chapter Five exposes these rules and the realities of organisations' internal processes designed to keep targets on the back foot. Equipped with an understanding of how organisations compound the harm and how and why complaints processes do not work (and are, in fact, not designed to) targets can better understand their options, and save themselves a good deal of time and aggravation.

Because management does not want to know, HR/P&C departments often stonewall and delay, with the result that complaints and investigations, not surprisingly, go nowhere. Processes supposedly created to assist targets actually silence them through non-disclosure agreements and inappropriate procedures, tactics such as outrage management and DARVO (Deny, Attack, Reverse Victim and Offender) and more.

Targets have the dubious distinction of playing a complex leading role in workplace abuse pantomime. That role includes being punished, tacitly and insidiously, by both the abuse and its aftermath. A safe learning organisation would welcome the opportunity to recognise a problem, resolve it and change for the better. The Japanese concept of kaizen, a 'continuous improvement' system, demonstrates this manner of valuing employee input.

'Complaints culture' casts the target worker as the misfit troublemaker who doesn't belong. Target workers might start out thinking they are doing the right thing by coming forward, only to find themselves confused, destabilised and demoralised by the internal processes of the organisation. Institutional betrayal is often more traumatising than the abuse itself.

The reality is that the target is not the source of the problem, as is often claimed, but rather a sentinel species in a toxic environment. Harassment must be recognised and addressed as a shared challenge with a collective responsibility to change. It is no longer tenable for management to pronounce that harassment is wrong, while at the same time looking the other way, with the refrain that 'it is not our problem'. In today's cubicled coal mines, however, targets are not thanked for alerting others to danger. They are cast instead as organisational heretics. To be the sentinel is both unwitting and unwelcome.

As Chapter Four explained, though management inaction breaches an employer's legal responsibilities, workers rarely have the wherewithal to bring legal action. They have little choice but to rely on the organisation's internal processes and the compounding betrayal that comes with it. Inaccessible, ineffective processes disempower targets. As Lyndon B. Johnson famously observed, 'You win a battle by not losing it.' In this Chapter, we consider the many ways in which the internal processes around psychological harassment, supposedly designed to assist in curtailing the abuse, actually reinforce target disadvantage and the conditions for abuse to thrive. Sometimes a tiny ripple of hope seems like a big ask.

Coming to terms with where you stand and what you can expect

Assessing the situation realistically, what can targets do in response to harassment? Given its prevalence and the high toll it exacts from individuals, teams, organisations, families and society, one might expect targets to feel confident to call it out, that they could count on the support of employers, managers and colleagues to stop the epidemic of workplace psychological harassment. Unfortunately, that's not the case.

To come forward and report workplace psychological harassment is not a simple or easy decision. The issue presents what can seem like a bleak outlook, and it is a problem that requires all of us to work to change. Until we all accept accountability and get behind the needed change, the burden is primarily on targets to do the hard work.

Targets must be realistic when considering what action to take. When carried out intentionally, with measures to ensure their own safety and well-being, this decision process can be empowering, and it can save months, even years, of confusion, pain and anxiety. Sensible, durable decisions require as much information and understanding as possible about the true nature of the situation. A key aspect of this is realising that their interests and those of their employer are not aligned and that colleagues, even those counted as friends, are also likely to turn against them.

Many of us believe that management genuinely cares about cleaning up bad behaviour. However, often, management chooses to avoid exposing themselves and the organisation to the expense and risk of criticism and scrutiny. As discussed in Chapter Four, their interests are often more aligned with those of the perpetrator than the target.

As targets are left to shoulder the burden alone, in the face of what seems a perverse process of vilification and blame, organisations and bystanders alike discredit and turn against them. As the process unfolds, it seems there is only one thing a target can be sure of - this is not the workplace they thought they knew. Core beliefs upon which they once relied are questioned, and targets are left wondering how to make sense of it all.

> *In essence, the system ...is run by workplace bullies for the benefit of workplace bullies and is designed to suppress and disenfranchise any worker who dares challenge the status quo.*
> Submission 34

Assessing options and making a plan

Very often, the issue of harassment is framed as the target's problem, despite the weight of research that shows it is an organisational and social issue. It is up to management to stop it. However, according to the current organisational/managerial procedural dictates, if there is a problem, targets have no choice but to respond as though it is their problem because management frames it that way, i.e. the target needs to learn to become better equipped to deal with it.

> *The (Department) has advised me to seek strategies from the psychologist to deal with bullying...*
>
> Submission 285

There is no straightforward path for targets. Abuse impacts people, relationships, and work environments differently. The workplace can become a battleground or a desert where people live underground and interact furtively to avoid the toxic environment's influence and stain.

In this context, a target faces the difficult decision to speak up against the abuse. It is a true dilemma, the choice between walking away and having to find a new job and start over, often with a demotion or pay cut...or engaging in what often becomes a devastating confrontation. We know that for a target to complain invites further abuse and betrayal. The organisation's response can be worse than the harassment itself - one of many reasons why targets commonly choose not to report or file complaints.

Targets may be advised, like many other victims of abuse, to 'take it on the chin, don't be so sensitive' or 'it's nothing, don't be a whinger'. Though in some places, there has been a move to celebrate workers who speak up about abuse as emotionally aware, competent, loyal, upstanding people, this is not the prevailing attitude in Australian workplaces. The recent cases of Richard Boyle and David McBride highlight the general attitude to whistleblowing. Everything in our society says, 'Forget about it. Let it go.'

Even if a part of the target agrees that walking away is the best choice, another part of them screams, 'No, it's not fair. It's not right. It's important to stand up and fight this.' They are conflicted, knowing that trying to address the problem probably will not do any good, the chips are stacked against them, and they cannot do it alone. However, some still believe that speaking up is the right thing to do, that real equity (not just the brochure), teamwork, and transparency are things organisations want and can benefit from, and that positive change can actually happen. They think:

> *If we don't stand up and speak out, then nothing will change.*
>
> Submission 253

And so some targets try to be the person who bravely stands up for change, only to find that the harassment is just the start of what is too often a devastatingly challenging, sometimes soul-destroying journey. Assuming the target wants to stay in the job and confront the situation, they need the tools to manage on multiple levels, not only to bear the harassment but also to do the work needed to transform it. They must:

1. Defend against attacks that others don't or won't recognise.

2. Earn a bad reputation for fighting a battle others don't want any part of.

3. Continue to function 'normally' at their jobs, remaining productive and positive, a part of 'the team' despite being targeted, isolated and vilified. Essentially, this means enduring the hypocrisy of the pretence that everything is fine in order to be seen as being positive team members, not 'whingers', complainers, or whistleblowers.

4. Collect, assemble and prepare irrefutable evidence to seek some action through whatever processes might be available, even though organisational complaints, investigation, and legal processes are pitted against them, time-consuming, and emotionally and financially draining, all in what feels like a Herculean and vain effort to have the problem recognised and addressed.

5. Manage the cognitive dissonance and stress of this burden, and maintain physical, mental, emotional and spiritual well-being and resilience against the odds. Targets require the focus of an elite athlete to cope with the struggle to maintain a normal life, to look after themselves and their loved ones and not be physically and psychologically destroyed by the harassment, compounded by the perverse processes and professional and financial damage.

The target needs a plan to meet these multiple challenges by assessing how much they need to protect their own well-being and weighing that against how much they are willing to sacrifice to move the dial a little toward change. These two objectives are not the same thing. In some ways, standing up to abuse is good for our well-being. It helps confirm our values, our boundaries and our agency. On the other hand, activism for a safer workplace can come at a high cost, and, as we have noted, we do not yet live in a world that cherishes whistleblowers, as Jennifer Freyd of the Center for Institutional Courage advocates. So, targets must evaluate what is safe for their health and well-being and find the right balance for them to deal with a situation they never wanted or intended, that has befallen them against their wishes.

Avenues available to targets to try to resolve the matter include:

- approaching the perpetrator directly
- seeking assistance from the employer through internal processes and
- legal redress.

All of these have the potential to achieve results; however, there are some considerable impediments to the efficacy of each. Legal and other professionals can help assess on an ongoing basis how to move forward as things evolve.

At first, many targets may not recognise harassment for what it is, but once they do, they are already weakened, destabilised, gaslighted and/or otherwise undermined. Even when the behaviour is clearly recognisable as harassment, targets may not know how to talk about it, may not have a trusted colleague to confide in (particularly true for minorities, new staff, etc.), want to belong, think people will not understand or think nothing can be done, believe they deserve it. Targets may feel embarrassed or not want to appear weak.

According to the principle of subsidiarity, in the first instance, the target should speak with the perpetrator. Some experts support the view that people who abuse may genuinely not recognise where they're doing, and with help, they can learn to behave differently. This is a worthy and optimistic view. In my experience, the target is likely to have tried this without success. Where direct communication by the target to the perpetrator can be effective, its greatest potential is very early. Direct action with the perpetrator is high risk and can easily lead to retaliation and escalation. As Gary Namie of the Workplace Bullying Institute observes, 'To tell people to confront the bully is about as ludicrous as to tell them to go to HR.'

A second option is to speak to someone else in the organisation, perhaps starting with a complaints officer. Some benefits may be gained if the target can garner useful information in the process. Further action within the organisation may include reporting/filing a complaint.

Targets who report or file complaints about emotionally abusive behaviour step into a new persona; they become the dreaded whistleblower. They are the ones calling out what others - for so many good reasons – have been unwilling to. Reporting and the process that ensues can bring significant personal stress, emotional strain and consequences that may include:

- retaliation in the form of undermining, gaslighting, isolating, harassment, intimidation, demotion and/or termination
- damage to their professional reputation, making it difficult to find future employment opportunities. They may be viewed as disloyal or untrustworthy, leading to stigmatization
- disruption of personal relationships, anxiety, and feelings of isolation or loss of trust in others; and
- legal risks.

Employees who report harassment often find themselves lacking support from colleagues, superiors, and even friends and family who may not understand or sympathize with their actions, further exacerbating the emotional toll. And, as we have seen, the organisation's weight is against it. Complaints processes take time, and outcomes vary. This uncertainty can be emotionally draining and leave targets questioning the utility of their actions.

> *I knew that by making a grievance, my career would not progress within my organisation. I was right. I now don't get interviewed for any promotion positions, even though I have recently completed a Masters of Management. It's as if I'm the shunned one – because I spoke out. I have watched other staff with less qualification, management experience, and business acumen – be promoted – whilst I am moved sideways.*
>
> Submission 289

The decision to speak up should be carefully considered, preferably with professional (including legal) counsel and support.

'... it was complicated by the fact that some of those to whom she was required to complain about bullying, were the people whose behaviour was the cause of the complaint.'
Submission 270

HR/P&C accountability and motivations

Internal processes are to targets of harassment what crevasses are to mountain climbers. The dangers are hidden, but potentially lethal to navigate. A target expects the organisation's internal complaints processes to be accessible, effective and fair. However, complaints processes are controlled by HR/P&C, which is accountable to management, and management benefits from stonewalling and ineffective processes. Internal processes are designed to silence. So another belief targets would do well to ditch sooner rather than later is thinking they can rely on HR/P&C for help. Just as they believed the employer would be motivated to stop the harassment, naïve targets often think they will have HR/P&C support. The overwhelming evidence is that they do not. Therefore, targets must be prepared to navigate processes designed to protect the status quo.

...don't kid yourself that they [HR] are impartial.
Submission 289

HR/P&C departments are responsible for setting and upholding policies, mediating conflicts, and ensuring fair treatment. They are also there to help hire and retain good talent, help deal with underperformance, and administer employee benefits and compensation. They help establish and maintain culture; this includes responding to employee concerns, answering questions, suggesting courses of action. All of this is in their remit. However, their first and foremost responsibility is to minimise risk and legal liability for the organisation. They have limited influence or decision-making power, particularly in company policy matters, management decisions, or organisational change.

Human Resources loyalties are with senior management, not individual targets of harassment, and so their actions tend to preserve the status quo. (HR/P&C speak about 'change management' is something else entirely.) They may say they want better workplace culture; they may even call themselves something like 'People and Culture', 'People Experience' or 'Talent Management'. Whatever the name, however, they are still widely perceived as biased, favouring management rather than advocating for employees.

> *There is too much trust placed in these officers... and very little accountability. When a matter is reported directly... the response is usually 'are you sure that is what happened?'.... mates investigating mates.*
> Submission 282

Undoubtedly, there are HR/P&C departments which are sensitive to their obligations and carry out their duties in an exemplary fashion. However, it is not uncommon for HR/P&C personnel who are comfortable with the organisational hierarchy to support the perpetrator (who not infrequently ranks higher than they do). Because management does not want a fuss, because speaking up threatens the status quo, and because a problem not recognised or responded to is not a problem, HR/P&C is typically incentivised to sweep things under the rug.

> *...where there is a secretive, insular and insecure culture, Human Resources is likely to engage in unscrupulous actions to cover for and protect senior management from hassles, scrutiny and accountability.*
> Submission 252

The suspect terrain of internal procedures

'Informal' processes are often suggested to targets as a first option, for example, taking action directly, seeking advice from a supervisor, HR/P&C or union representative, or an equal opportunity contact person, or requesting that the employer address the situation. 'Informal complaints' may be resolved without investigation by bringing the two sides together to conciliate. This can be appropriate in cases where the allegations are less serious or the problem is based on miscommunication or a misunderstanding.

While 'informal' procedures are supposed to be useful for quick problem-solving, the obstacles are substantial and the results uncertain. Managers may lack the skills to handle early intervention. Too often, the very interventions ostensibly designed to help and empower targets lead to further destabilisation. An informal process is less likely to be appropriate in situations where there is:

- a series of complaints about the same person, or

- a risk of repeated conduct.
- concern about cultural or systemic issues.
- a risk to the reputation of the organisation; or
- a wider public interest in the matters that are being raised.

It is estimated that between two-thirds to three-quarters of targets do not report. Roughly a similar percentage of targets end up leaving. Without the will in the organisation to change the workplace culture, the target has less chance to resolve harassment successfully.

Clear explanation is often lacking with respect to what the complaints process entails (ditto investigation, conciliation and mediation). It is not in the employer's interest for a complainant to clearly understand the process. Vague processes can be adjusted to suit their purposes and to keep the target on the back foot, confused about what's going on and less able to act effectively.

A 2017 survey showed that a third of those who experienced harassment expressed a lack of faith in the complaints process. The most common reason given for not reporting, from approximately half the respondents, was that 'it would have made it worse for me'.

> *If you go and see them and report anything then they will find out and make life hell or sack you for no specific reason anyway. So, what's the use??*
>
> Submission 276

It's even worse if you're a casual...

> *And who are you going to report these issues to?? Nobody will be prepared to support you because their job is on the line. More senior management has your word against theirs – and guess what? You're not even a permanent staff member!! So, you have no rights as a casual against a Senior Manager who has been ensconced for 8 or 10 years.*
>
> Submission 276

<u>Weighing the benefits and risks of filing a complaint</u>

The calculus of options is not static for individuals considering making a complaint. And as conditions change, the uncertainty will further destabilise the target's well-being. It is essential for individuals considering making a complaint to count up the potential rewards and risks and to seek advice to navigate the process effectively. Doing this early in the process helps avoid mistakes that could prove costly or damaging later.

The first risk is that the complaints process puts responsibility/accountability on the target, often portrayed as the offender through DARVO or similar tactics. If the perpetrator is held accountable, if the organisation does change a little, will this benefit the target or attract resentment? When we suggest someone else change, how grateful are they?

The complaint process is usually a protracted affair that wears the target down emotionally and physically, risking depression and worse, during which the target is firmly entrenched in the victim role and, at the same time, blamed and stigmatised in the workplace. It's reasonable to expect further damage to reputation and career, loss of goodwill, loss of opportunities to collaborate within the organisation, and potential job loss. There are family stressors, friendship costs, and damaged relationships.

> *Case law is littered with examples of employees raising complaints (to their manager about a colleague or raising a complaint about their own manager to a more senior manager) and the complaint being ignored or investigated poorly.*
>
> Submission 100

Potential rewards include the possibility that the perpetrator might be held accountable, the chance the organisation might improve — and a remote possibility that the target might receive some compensation. Targets may hope to be able to stay in the job. Unfortunately, unless things change, this will be a toxic work environment, possibly even more toxic than before.

We rely on targets to lodge complaints but punish them for doing so. So, people just walk away. And these painful and damaging patterns persist. It is costly to the organisation and the individuals within it. At the same time, we continue to pay lip service to mental well-being and healthy workplaces. And wonder why people are cynical.

Complaints process sabotage

Targets need to understand that the process itself is typically designed to carry out the ends of management, as implemented by HR/P&C. Don't recognise, don't respond ... Complaints processes can sometimes feel like institutionalised hypocrisy, reinforcing management control and obscuring intransigence in curtailing harassment. Employers and their HR/P&C departments say all the right things and seem concerned with preventing and stopping harassment while not doing so. And voila! Complaints process camouflage.

> *As practiced practised today, the state of discrimination, abuse and bullying are totally unsatisfactory, with no effective corrective processes.*
>
> Submission 31

Putting the effort behind the lie, rather than the remedy, the organisation gives the impression of compliance in meeting its legal duty to provide a safe working environment, while in fact providing little more than the appearance of confronting harassment. Policies and procedures are managerial tools to control employees, reflecting the power structures that protect management rather than solve the problem. Sometimes, the complaints process can even serve as a sort of Trojan horse that allows HR/P&C to obtain all the target's information while revealing none of their own.

HR/P&C is often unresponsive and/or slow to address matters. Targets wait weeks, even months, to get a reply to a simple email. This can create frustration and the perception that HR/P&C is not prioritizing employee well-being or actively working to resolve issues.

> *The University has never been proactive and would rather deny the existence of a problem, frequently not responding to emails.*
>
> Submission 280

But that's not all. The following excerpt lists a range of other ways HR/P&C departments betray workers who report harassment:

> *Some examples of shady conduct carried out by Human Resources against complainants ...include:*
>
> - *claiming complainants cannot remain at their workplace (sometimes based on dubious grounds) and degradingly parading complainants out of the workplace under guard or noticeable supervision, like a criminal.*

- cutting pass access of complainants without telling them so that the complainants are put in a publicly humiliating circumstance when they discover for the first time, in front of their colleagues, that their pass has been disabled.
- misusing confidential information in complainants' personal files against complainants, such as medical records.
- hiring private investigators to 'investigate' complainants without the complainants' knowledge (which is more akin to spying).
- secretly briefing complainants' perpetrators and their perpetrators' supporters and divulging personal information about the complainants. secretly briefing complainants' medical practitioners to try to influence the medical practitioners' diagnoses and prognoses in favour of the APS agency's agenda.manipulating or pressuring complainants to allow Human Resources personnel to attend the complainants' private consultations with their medical practitioners under the guise of 'care' and 'support' when really it is about Human Resources trying to fish for personal information about the complainants.
- compulsorily referring complainants to psychiatric examinations against the complainants' free will and providing the APS hired psychiatrists with inaccurate or wildly misleading information about the complainants.
- making threats against complainants, coercing complainants or misleading complainants (such as in relation to trying to have complainants sign documents that are not in the complainants' interests).
- failing to engage in impartial fact-finding processes.
- disingenuously characterising workplace mistreatment as a 'miscommunication', 'misunderstanding' or a 'mere personality clash'....
- soliciting personal information from complainants.
- engaging in fraudulent cover-up.

Submission 252

HR/P&C departments can be perceived as being more concerned with avoiding legal issues than fostering a positive work environment. Legal advisors stress the importance of not making concessions or admissions at any stage of the process to avoid invoking any legal redress, including commercial exposure. This 'insurance framework' only serves to perpetuate and sanction workplace harassment.

Two employees left the organisation as a direct result of his bullying. One of them noted on their exit form/ delivered to the Human Relations (HR) area, stated words to the effect of 'I am leaving the organisation as a direct result of senior management's failure to stop bullying and harassment In the property area'. This was ignored by HR. Many complaints were made to HR regarding this fellow's behaviour, but all were ignored, with the contact in HR saying words to the effect of 'you will need to learn how to communicate better'.

Submission 37

Tactics to obfuscate, delay and frustrate proper process

Employers and HR/P&C departments feign support for preventing and stopping harassment in many ways:

- maintaining a strongly worded workplace harassment policy for show only.

- confidentially acknowledging an employee's concerns about harassment, pretending to support and investigate, but deliberately taking no action in anticipation that they will lose interest and/or resign.

- minimising harassment to a potentially lesser issue, such as a personality clash or a misinterpretation of reasonable management practice.

- avoiding formal investigation that is potentially costly and reputation-damaging for the employer.

- offering confidential processes such as mediation as a means of disposing of the matter because it is cheaper, faster and easier to control, as well as reinforcing that the harassment in question is not an organisational problem but rather a conflict between two parties and putting a greater burden on the target.

- withholding information and advice from an employee about how to prepare a formal harassment complaint and/or change the procedures so that allegations, if made, are poorly presented and easier to defend against or dismiss.

- intimidating an employee who asks to discuss their harassment confidentially by inviting them to an 'ambush meeting' with multiple HR/P&C representatives, managers, sometimes including the alleged perpetrator, and/or the employer's lawyer.

- conducting a sham investigation of an employee's allegations with a predetermined 'unsubstantiated' outcome.
- making or implying the possibility of a false misconduct/harassment accusation against a complainant to discourage them from pursuing their grievance further.
- discrediting the allegations during the investigation process by using aggressive cross-examination techniques, bureaucratic language, and obscurely worded or trick questions to confuse and intimidate the complainant.
- ignoring, delaying, or refusing requests to provide information to a complainant about the progress of an investigation and/or deliberately delaying notifying them about the outcome to exacerbate their stress and anxiety, thus putting additional pressure on them to withdraw their complaint or resign.
- skewing minutes of meetings to make the complainant seem unreasonable and minimise the complaint, making it seem insignificant or groundless.
- providing ambiguous progress reports during an investigation to imply that things are not going the complainant's way.
- delaying decision-making on an internal investigation to keep a complainant in a state of distress, putting them under financial pressure to withdraw their complaint, return to work or resign, thus voiding their complaint.
- accusing the employee of making a vexatious (false/mischievous) complaint, being a troublemaker or that their complaint constitutes misconduct for which the employer is considering taking disciplinary or legal action.
- secretly overturn an investigator's finding that favours the complainant;.placing false or misleading entries in a complainant's personnel file to discredit them, including records of meetings or conversations that never took place, especially about bogus performance or disciplinary concerns; and/or
- requiring the target to continue under untenable working conditions, including continuing to work with/report to the alleged perpetrator.

> *I tried to stand up against it, but employers like mine purport to need a smoking gun- no, not one, they need at least a dozen smoking guns and even then, they'd probably say 'nothing to see here'.*
>
> *It's not the evidence they lack, it's the motivation.*
>
> *A month after I received an email that my complaint had been closed, a former co-worker contacted me to say she had filed a complaint and had been told no complaints had ever been filed prior to hers. A blatant lie.*
>
> Personal diary

Complaints processes serve management objectives to deny there is a problem; or if a problem must be recognised, not to respond; or if they must respond, to portray the matter as a non-issue, just a conflict between the perpetrator, whom they support tacitly or otherwise, and the target, portrayed as a troublemaker.

Though, like management, HR/P&C may say the right things and seem concerned with preventing and stopping harassment, complaint processes can be inadequate, often counterproductive, to the point that they are even more damaging than the harassment itself.

Complaints culture and processes together obstruct healthy conflict management

Targets are highly motivated to stop harassment, but we know targets commonly decide not to file complaints. Of the many reasons for this, the nature of the process itself is a key deterrent. The complaints culture and internal processes of resolution - including negotiation, mediation, and investigation - can be more damaging than the harassment that led to them, obstructing healthy conflict management and transformation in a variety of ways:

- Complaints culture obstructs effective and fair resolution because it absolves management and the organisation of accountability. It replaces accountability with blame, the dyadic dodge that shifts responsibility from the organisation, where it belongs, to the target /perpetrator relationship.

- The complaints machinery obstructs healthy conflict management and transformation by keeping the burden on the target to fix it. Targets are already harmed and weakened psychologically by the abuse at the hands of the harasser. In particular, their self-confidence is undermined, so they cannot plan and respond effectively. They also rarely have the requisite time, money and psychosocial resources.

- Placing all responsibility on targets to speak up and follow up traps targets in a posture of angry, urgent petulance and amplifies their isolation, feeding into the process of DARVO and providing a rationale for the employer to label them as troublemakers, disloyal whistleblowers.

- Complaints processes aggravate 'victim mentality', keeping the target in the victim role, as the process requires repeating, reliving and thinking about presenting the case in hopes of justice. The last thing the target needs is to rehearse over and over what has happened, relive it, and inhabit it for months and years through a maze-like charade of putative response processes.

- Harassment typically involves a power imbalance, where the perpetrator holds a position of authority or influence over the target. This power dynamic can make targets feel vulnerable and powerless. Unless it actively compensates for this imbalance, the complaints process favours the perpetrator and fails at the outset to adequately address a key aspect of the harassment interaction.

- The evidence targets are expected to produce can be difficult, even impossible, to document, especially since much of the behaviour can be subtle or through omission.

- Bystanders may be reluctant to corroborate due to perceived risks to their own positions and/or because bystanders, co-workers and managers are often turned against targets, further weakening and demoralising them and detracting further from their capacity to respond.

- The complaints process puts the target in a position of supplicant, further eroding the target's sense of agency and confidence. This not only concerns the interaction with the perpetrator, management, and the complaints process but also concerns colleagues and other bystanders. While beseeching others for help with little hope of success, the complaints process keeps targets in the injury and exacerbates their victimisation.

- At the same time that it exacerbates the victimisation of the target, the process infantilises the perpetrator, who also relies on the process, reducing the already remote possibility of resolution between the parties, even if inherent disadvantages of the resolution process, such as power and balance were to be addressed with skilled professional help.

- Infantilising the target and the perpetrator, complaints culture puts management in the position of controlling, narcissistic parents who only care about how events reflect upon their reputation.

- Complaints culture obstructs healthy conflict management and transformation because employees who experience workplace psychological harassment will hesitate to come forward due to fear of retaliation. They may worry about negative consequences, such as further harassment, reputation damage, or even job loss. This fear can discourage individuals from reporting incidents of harassment, leading to underreporting and a lack of trust in the complaints process.

- Concerns about confidentiality in the complaints process can deter individuals from filing complaints. If they perceive that their identity or the details of the complaint will not be kept confidential, they may be reluctant, fearing negative consequences or privacy breaches.

- Complaints processes can be time-consuming, involving multiple stages and procedures. Delays in resolution can lead to frustration and a sense that the process is ineffective in addressing the immediate impact of harassment on the target's well-being and work environment.

- When complainants do not receive clear and timely updates on the progress of their complaints, it can contribute to a perception of opacity and uncertainty. This lack of transparency can erode confidence in the process and discourage individuals from coming forward or pursuing their complaints.

- When the outcomes of the complaints process do not result in appropriate actions to address emotionally abusive behaviour and prevent its recurrence, the perception develops that the process is ineffective in resolving issues and improving the workplace environment.

Perhaps most important is that a culture of complaints is fundamentally founded upon negativity, from a premise of 'what is wrong?' instead of 'how can we improve?'. Proceeding from the assumption of what is wrong encourages the dance of deflection to persist, where no one is willing to accept the tarnish. At the same time, because the fundamental premise of complaint is the fact of a wrong, the process requires someone to be in the wrong. The simple (perverse) solution? Blame the target.

First, the target is harmed and then must bear the burden of calling out and changing harassment, while employers and bystanders label them as complainers, whingers, or whistleblowers and close ranks against them. Targets bear the burden of preventing and stopping workplace psychological harassment in the face of opposition from the perpetrator and the entire organisation through processes and procedures unsuitable for the purpose. Even where they might seem to have the potential to be effective, they are ineffective in implementation. What's a target to do...?

- Go talk to your manager? A good percentage of the time, they're the perpetrator.
- Talk to their manager? A good percentage of the time, they support the perpetrator.
- HR/P&C complaints, processes and procedures? Ditto.
- Legal avenues require time, money and psychological resources, and they carry their own risks and uncertain outcomes.

Complaint processes typically involve one person, isolated, crying out, 'Look - there's something wrong here!' Then DARVO kicks in and makes that person the problem. They are then shamed and stigmatised through processes such as mediation and investigation, carried out in secret. Targets are isolated, not just by the perpetrator but also by the organisation and the process, exponentially compounding the harm. Through DARVO and outrage management tactics, targets framed as the problem suffer the double whammy, first the effects of the harassment itself and then the effects of the employer response that can compromise targets' futures irreparably. Their careers, belief systems and personal lives are disrupted and damaged. And these are often people from marginalised groups who are already at a disadvantage in terms of equal opportunity, equal pay, retirement savings and superannuation.

> *So, the complaint remained unresolved, and I felt that they wanted it this way to show me and possibly others how staff who submit a complaint are treated. I felt intimidated and bullied by raising it again until recently for fear that it would cause more reprisals.*
>
> Submission 287

Navigating resolution mechanisms within complaints processes

Negotiation

Negotiation refers to a process of discussion and compromise in a balanced interaction where participants are willing and able to reach a mutually acceptable agreement. Negotiation requires equal power dynamics and a willingness to engage in good-faith discussions. In a harassment scenario of repeated mistreatment or intimidation, with the perpetrator exerting control or authority over the target, the power dynamics may prevent the target from negotiating on an equal footing.

Negotiation implies a degree of respect and professionalism that may not exist in a harassment situation. Workplace psychological harassment usually involves behaviours that are fundamentally inappropriate and unacceptable, such as verbal abuse, threats, or undermining the target's work. It can have serious emotional and psychological effects on the target. Negotiating directly with the perpetrator may escalate the situation or put the target at further risk when it is crucial to prioritize the safety and well-being of the target and seek appropriate interventions.

Because harassment is qualitatively different from conflict, framing harassment generically as conflict can only result in further damage to the target. The notion of shared responsibility is particularly troublesome in certain precepts of negotiation theory, such as 'separating the person from the problem'. In the case of harassment, the person is the problem and hence cannot be separated from it. Trying to frame the situation otherwise can only be disastrous for the target, who will experience the inability to do so as yet another failure on their part.

Mediation

Expecting targets to enter into agreements with their perpetrators constitutes a form of punishment to the targets.
Submission 252

Assuming there is an understanding of its limitations, mediation is a flexible tool, and it can be useful if carried out appropriately as an early intervention. HR/P&C departments tend to favour mediation as the least costly process and the easiest for them to control. However, there are challenges despite the potential value of mediation in the early stages. Mediation can often be anything but a consensual process, fair and balanced for all parties.

Also, many of the same issues are of concern here as for negotiation, for example, the psychological safety of the target and the inappropriate characterisation of the issue as conflict rather than abuse. As with negotiation, power imbalance can compromise the mediation process. Studies on mediation in hierarchical conflicts between supervisors and subordinates found that hierarchical position plays a crucial role in the mediation process and that the power imbalance persists in the mediation process. Thus, the combined effects of power imbalance, the inability to defend and the extensive undermining of the target's personal resources that characterise harassment relationships suggest that mediation may not only be inappropriate but harmful.

A basic assumption of mediation is that the parties to the dispute are sufficiently capable of negotiating with one another as relative equals. However, this is not the case where targets have been diminished and disempowered due to the harassment experience and are undermined in their abilities to be assertive in dealing directly with the actor. Further, the less powerful party is less willing to engage in direct processes such as mediation due to fear of retaliation and/or the perception that change is unlikely.

The emphasis on compromise and forward focus in resolving workplace psychological harassment is misguided. Mediation focuses not on the past but present and future relationships, which seems ideal for moving forward. However, it can fail to address past offences adequately. Because damage to the target is often cumulative in nature, the extent of the harm can easily be underestimated or delegitimised.

Harassment matters often require investigation, fact-finding, ownership and reconciliation. In workplace psychological harassment, where one person is clearly the victim, failure to address the past does little to address the target's concerns for justice and recognition of the harm done. The perpetrator may favour this approach because it does not require him or them to acknowledge responsibility for their actions. And anyone who has engaged in harassment should be offered help to change; even minor incidents can be growth opportunities.

The employer also benefits from obscuring past causes. A key part of the matter of workplace psychological harassment is not the harassment itself; it is the context that provides the environment for harassment to flourish that must be addressed before any real change can happen. Because organisational context is antecedent to workplace psychological harassment, the organisation should be included as a key participant.

I reflect further below on considerations around confidentiality in general. Confidentiality in mediation is a potential problem for targets. It silences the target when all they have is a voice, ceding control of the narrative to the perpetrator and the employer. Further, reinforcing secrecy does not help create a collaborative, transparent, cooperative engagement culture, and mediation may obscure harassment patterns in an organisation, particularly if case-by-case processing is used to cover up systematic or repeated violations. Mediation can be the process of choice for resolving harassment claims, but it provides no public record. Using a confidential process in cases where harassment has been established means that witnesses receive little or no information regarding the dispensation of the situation. Thus, an essential source of information enabling an organisation to take corrective action may be stifled and can reduce employee trust. It may contribute to the sense that the organisation tolerates these behaviours, reducing the likelihood of reporting harassment.

Rather than approaching workplace psychological harassment as an interpersonal dispute, it might better be treated as any other type of abuse, including a perpetrator and victim and invoking a process of fact-finding, reconciliation, reparation and related measures.

The target stands a better chance of fairness in mediation if there is a robust, transparent process and an impartial, versatile, knowledgeable, skilled and impartial mediator. The target is often not permitted to have a say in the selection process of a mediator, though this is a crucial aspect of the process. There are alternative mediation styles, techniques & hybrid forms of mediation practice, such as transformative and therapeutic mediation. Processes of mediating workplace psychological harassment can encompass admission of guilt, forgiveness and reconciliation. They can lead to relocating the target to another part of the organisation or removing the perpetrator from their job rather than the target from theirs. Such outcomes can only be available if the mediator's perspective is open to them.

> *HR informed me that a mediator had been selected. When I asked to see their qualifications, I was told that I did not have a right to have input into the selection process, and anyway, the perpetrator had already agreed to the choice of this mediator (!) These people are professionals. So I wonder - have they been operating in this fashion for so long that it no longer seems outrageous? Or are they enjoying rubbing my nose in it? Or do they just not care?*
>
> Personal diary

Investigation

A workplace investigation is a formal process to determine the facts of, document, and evaluate a complaint and recommend appropriate responses, including preventative measures. An investigation is said to provide the opportunity to make correct decisions, re-establish fairness, conclude the matter and signal to employees that these issues are being taken seriously.

The effectiveness of workplace investigations depends on various factors, including the investigator's expertise, the organisation's commitment to act on investigation findings, and the transparency of the process. Independent workplace investigations are, in theory, conducted by skilled, neutral investigators. Given that they are engaged and paid by the employer and managed through HR/P&C, however, it is unclear to what extent the investigator brings objectivity to their assessment of the situation. It is also worth considering that harassment is a subjective psychological phenomenon, while the investigative process is in theory objective.

Again, in theory, investigations provide an opportunity to comprehensively examine the alleged harassment incidents. Investigators can collect evidence, interview relevant parties, and review documentation to understand the situation thoroughly. The investigation report will typically outline the relevant facts, evidence and law. It will assess whether the events are proven and may evaluate whether the action was reasonable. It will make recommendations, including whether disciplinary action is warranted and suggestions for further training. Depending on the depth of the investigation, it can help uncover the root causes and extent of the behaviour and guide the development of appropriate workplace policies.

Workplace investigations demonstrate employer compliance with legal requirements regarding harassment complaints. They have the potential to reassure employees that their concerns are taken seriously and addressed through a thorough process. This can contribute to a happier, safer work environment through a restored sense of trust among colleagues. Appropriately handled, an investigation can promote civility moving forward and help rebuild trust within the organisation.

Workplace investigations often involve ensuring confidentiality for complainants, witnesses, and those accused of harassment. From a target's point of view, the investigation may offer the advantage of moving some of the onus to the investigator. However, the target will still need to provide detailed documentation.

> *Really, there is not much to gain for me, but rather, I feel it is the employer's decision. I thought they had a legal obligation to investigate…*
>
> Personal diary

Engaging an experienced, independent, external workplace investigator can help address the complaint promptly and transparently; deliver procedural fairness; ensure compliance with relevant legal and regulatory frameworks; avoid distracting managers from their core responsibilities; and minimise confusion and distraction of staff. However, the investigation brings its own set of risks and costs to the employer. It must be considered whether the investigation will be internal or external, the scope and duration, and how it will reflect the seriousness of the complaint or conduct and its potential consequences. And the investigation is not designed to implement solutions.

> *We rarely see an investigation process achieving a positive outcome. … it is generally very difficult for everyone involved…When something is six months, 12 months or longer down the path, and you have systemic, repeated behaviour, it becomes very, very difficult. You can have*

> *an investigation, and it can prove that this is the issue. That is great. Then what do you do with it? You still have an individual here and an individual here. You have been found to demonstrate harassment behaviours. What do you then do with that? The situation has not gone away by virtue of an investigation.*
>
> DTC submission

A formal investigation report will typically list the relevant facts at issue, balance those facts with evidence and law, and assess whether the events are proven, not proven, or inconclusive. If the situation involves managerial decision-making, the report will also detail whether that decision-making was reasonable or unreasonable. The report will typically end with recommendations for the employer, including whether disciplinary action is warranted, suggestions for further training, and the development of additional workplace policies.

> *Investigations into workplace bullying are invariably and almost universally inadequate.*
>
> Submission 35

An investigation is fact-finding and makes recommendations - it brings with it its own set of risks and is not designed to implement solutions. Some individuals may view investigations into harassment complaints as insufficient or biased. Trust in the process will be compromised if they are not thorough, impartial, or inclusive. On the other hand, if people are aware of them, investigations can indicate that the organisation does not tolerate harassment.

> *Understand what an investigation entails. It's a process. Takes ages. Nothing happens – usually. And then it's over. Awesome.*
>
> Personal diary

Who does confidentiality really protect?

Confidentiality provisions are supposed to protect participants in the process of resolution, and so they encourages targets to come forward without fear of reprisal, potentially leading to a more effective, open and honest complaints process. But confidentiality cuts both ways. Like all secrecy, confidentiality can conceal and engender error, injury, and abuse. There are limits, conflicts, and sometimes overriding considerations. In fact, it is hard to keep a complaint secret in a way that protects the target or limits reprisals, and the balance between the benefits of transparency versus the protections of confidentiality can be difficult to achieve.

Targets should consider that confidentiality protects the perpetrator and the organisation from unsavoury publicity, limiting rumours about managers and awareness of the prevalence of complaints. Confidentiality also obscures awareness and shrouds the involvement of bystanders and others. At least as much as it protects, confidentiality can exacerbate harm, perpetuate the problem, and block any feedback loop about what has occurred. It is said that information is power, but it is worth asking whose interests that power serves, and whose interests are compromised by lack of transparency? The deprivation of the capacity to access and use information disempowers. Targets must consider whether agreeing to confidentiality is right for them or whether the freedom to speak might serve them better.

Recent legislation in the US, the 'Silenced No More Act', SB331, in California, reflects what was learned from processes of addressing sexual harassment in the workplace. It prohibits employers from using confidentiality and non-disparagement clauses to silence workers who wish to speak about harassment or discrimination experienced during their employment.

Chapter conclusion

Experts say it is best if psychological harassment issues can be resolved early. Internal resolution is one of the very few options available to a target; however, mobbing, the dyadic dodge, DARVO, outrage management and the complaints culture, all affect internal resolution of a complaint. Targets can be significantly disadvantaged by all of these, and by the strategies and tactics of HR/P&C that often seem designed to deny or camouflage the harassment and sabotage processes to address it.

This chapter has also outlined the basic attributes of some commonly used resolution tools within the complaints processes, such as negotiation, mediation, and investigation. These are versatile tools that can potentially yield results but also carry risks. Finally, the chapter briefly explains the considerations surrounding confidentiality in harassment matters.

We might wish it were otherwise, but for now, there is no escaping the conclusion that organisational complaints processes can frustrate and damage targets. Legal recourse may be another option, but it, too, has its challenges, as the next chapter explains.

Selected references

Bok, S. (1983). The *limits of confidentiality*. Hastings Center Report.

Hodgins, M., MacCurtain, S., & Mannix-McNamara, P. (2020). Power and inaction: Why organizations fail to address workplace bullying. *International Journal of Workplace Health Management, 13*(3), 265-290.

Lutgen-Sandvik, P., & Sypher, B. D. (Eds.). (2010). *Destructive organizational communication: Processes, consequences, and constructive ways of organizing*. Routledge.

McDermott, M. J., & Garofalo, J. (2004). When advocacy for domestic violence victims backfires: Types and sources of victim disempowerment. *Violence against women, 10*(11), 1245-1266.

Newton, K.M. (2008). *Modern Literature and the Tragic*, Edinburg University Press.

Orifici, A. (2019). Unsystematic and unsettled: A map of the legal dimensions of workplace investigations in Australia. *The University of New South Wales Law Journal, 42*(3), 1075-1105.

Spencer, E. (2021). Mediating workplace bullying: A reflective case study. *Australasian Dispute Resolution Journal, 31*(2), 114-121.

Sullivan, K., & Osterman, K. (2010). *Bullying in the Irish workplace: A cause for concern*. Indirect and Direct Aggression; Österman, K., Ed.; Peter Lang Publishing: Frankfurt am Main.

https://legalvision.com.au/workplace-investigation/.

https://news.griffith.edu.au/2017/03/27/bullying-and-harassment-in-the-workplace-australian-universities/.

https://silencednomore.org/the-silenced-no-more-act. See also https://www.institutionalcourage.org/resources-for-changemakers.

https://www.aph.gov.au/Parliamentary_Business/Committees/House_of_Representatives_Committees?url=ee/bullying/report/chapter3.htm#anc13 3.131.

https://www.bosswhispering.com/Stop-the-Suffering.pdf.

Chapter Six

The legal landscape

Where there is no law, there is no freedom.
John Locke

Chapter Introduction

Given the challenges of internal resolution, legal recourse might seem a more promising option to address the issue. In any given jurisdiction, there are usually multiple regulations and legal theories on which to base a claim. Very often, however, there is much to be ventured for a slim possibility of only modest gain. Legal battles are risky as well as financially and emotionally draining.

This chapter provides an overview of anti-harassment legislation globally, a closer look at the legal avenues available to a target in Australia, and tips for any target considering legal action. If internal processes are not responsive or effective and if targets do not give up and leave, as a large percentage do, they may wish to defend their rights legally, a process which will require substantial emotional and financial resources. The options here can prove surprisingly limited, depending on the jurisdiction and the facts of any given situation.

A brief look at law and regulation around the world

While many countries have laws against sexual harassment, fewer have implemented legislation against workplace psychological harassment. As discussed briefly in Chapter Two, harassment is regarded differently depending on social and cultural context. Even in any country or jurisdiction, behaving well is notoriously difficult to legislate.

US Supreme Court Justice Potter Stewart's famous quote, 'I know it when I see it.' from *Jacobellis v Ohio* underscores the importance of non-rational elements in legal decision-making around civil norms, including civility in the workplace. Just as the US Supreme Court struggled with the definition of pornography in 1964, today, the lack of clarity around what is and is not workplace psychological abuse, including harassment, is problematic. 'I know it when I see it' may be true; nevertheless, it is a phrase that has been more criticised than lauded. Nonrational, intuitive and self-referential, it failed to provide the necessary guiding framework.

Similarly, to define what is and is not workplace psychological harassment and emotional abuse presents a challenge but a crucial one. As we noted at the start of this book, preventing and stopping workplace psychological abuse requires some shared understanding of what it is we are seeking to curtail. Definitions in the scholarly literature vary across disciplines and jurisdictions. Because developing an understanding of workplace psychological abuse is (and is not) very much about what society at any given place and time agrees upon, organisational and legal rules and processes need to be structured accordingly.

Efforts to address these issues vary across jurisdictions, and it is essential to consider the specific legislation, policies, and support systems in each country to understand their level of activity in combating workplace mistreatment. The legal definitions and implications of various forms of workplace psychological harassment vary depending on the jurisdiction. In some cases, certain forms of psychological abuse may be considered criminal offences, or addressed through workplace policies and regulations.

Around the world, some legislation has been implemented to prevent and address workplace emotional abuse, harassment, and/or mobbing such as the following as of the time of writing:

- Concerning European regulation of bullying/mobbing/harassment at work, no definition of bullying at work has been arrived at in the European Union (EU), and no specific European-wide legislative provisions refer explicitly to bullying at work. However, numerous European countries have enacted laws defining and prohibiting workplace bullying and mobbing, including France, Sweden, Norway, Finland, Denmark, Belgium, the Netherlands, Switzerland, and Serbia. Sweden, in particular, has been recognised for its progressive approach to workplace issues, including emotional abuse and bullying. The Swedish Work Environment Act obligates employers to take measures to prevent and address workplace harassment. Sweden also has well-established systems for reporting and investigating workplace incidents and support services for affected individuals.

- The United Kingdom has demonstrated some recognition of workplace psychological abuse as a serious issue. There, the Equality Act 2010 protects against harassment, including bullying, based on protected characteristics such as race, gender, or disability, and organisations are encouraged to have policies and procedures in place to prevent and address workplace bullying.

- In Canada, provinces such as Ontario, Quebec, and Manitoba have specific legislation that addresses workplace harassment, including psychological harm. Canada also has human rights commissions and tribunals that handle complaints related to workplace harassment and discrimination.

- Many US states have introduced or are considering workplace psychological safety legislation. The proposed Massachusetts law, for example, not only makes abuse illegal without protected status but also proactively addresses psychological violence with measures that require employers to ensure a safe work environment. US legislation empowers targets by allowing targets to file restraining orders, call for investigations, pursue civil and criminal actions against individuals and employers, and publicly disclose outcomes. Reporting and training requirements further emphasize the need for employers to acknowledge, monitor, and prevent psychological abuse.

- New Zealand's Health and Safety at Work Act 2015 obligates employers to ensure the health and safety of their workers, including addressing psychological harm. The country also has the Employment Relations Authority, which handles employment-related disputes, including bullying and harassment cases.

It is beyond the scope of this volume to go into global regulation in any detail, and as with all regulations, are subject to change at any time. It is best to check the legal information and advice providers for the particular jurisdiction for current information. That said, as an example, the following section provides a brief overview of the current state of play in the legal landscape of Australia.

Law and regulation in Australia

All Australian jurisdictions protect workers against workplace psychological harassment by a patchwork legislative and regulatory frameworks encompassing replacement health and safety (WHS) and other industrial legislation, anti-discrimination, and criminal and common law. There may also be workers' compensation when protections fail. However, none provides an 'all in one' response to workplace harassment, universal protection and recourse. Rather, they are overlapping frameworks, which can be confusing, frustrating and costly. The variation across states and territories adds to the difficulty.

Workers may wish to start by seeking assistance from one or more of several Commonwealth agencies that field enquiries and complaints about workplace bullying, harassment, victimisation and/or discrimination:

- The Australian Human Rights Commission (for human rights matters)
- The Fair Work Commission and Fair Work Ombudsman (for workplace rights matters)
- Safe Work Australia (for work health and safety matters)
- The Office of the Australian Information Commissioner (for privacy and FOI matters)
- The Australian Public Service Commission (for APS review matters)
- Comcare (for workplace injury matters)
- The Commonwealth Ombudsman (for administrative action matters)

There are also state and territory agencies for workplace health and safety:

- WorkSafe Victoria
- SafeWork SA

- WorkSafe Tasmania
- WorkSafe ACT
- SafeWork NSW
- Workplace Health and Safety/Worksafe Queensland
- WorkSafe WA
- NTWorkSafe

There are also State and Territory Human Rights and anti-discrimination agencies:

- Victoria Equal Opportunity and Human Rights Commission
- South Australia Equal Opportunity Commission
- Tasmania Office of the Anti-Discrimination Commissioner
- Australian Capital Territory Human Rights Commission
- New South Wales Anti-Discrimination Board
- Queensland Anti-Discrimination Commission
- Western Australia Equal Opportunity Commission
- Northern Territory Anti-Discrimination Commission

Many investigation/review agencies generally have limited jurisdiction and are under-resourced. Therefore, complainants may not receive the full assistance they require and processing their complaints may take considerable time. Unfortunately, many complaints can be drawn out for months, even years, adding to complainants' frustrations and suffering.

Submission 252

Legislated and common law approaches to address workplace psychological harassment are, at best, a patchwork. Targets of workplace psychological harassment may struggle to identify a sustainable course of action or cause of action that fits within the parameters of a particular regulation.

Workplace bullying is... poorly understood in the community, and the variety of approaches and definitions in different jurisdictions make it difficult for both employers and individual workers to understand their rights and responsibilities. Further, the overlap and distinction between workplace bullying, employment law (via the Fair Work Act 2009) and unlawful discrimination (in all jurisdictions) adds complexity.

Submission 185

The following 'triage' chart shows the main alternatives possible for a claim related to bulling. While it is based on conduct in Victoria, the options would be similar in other states and territories.

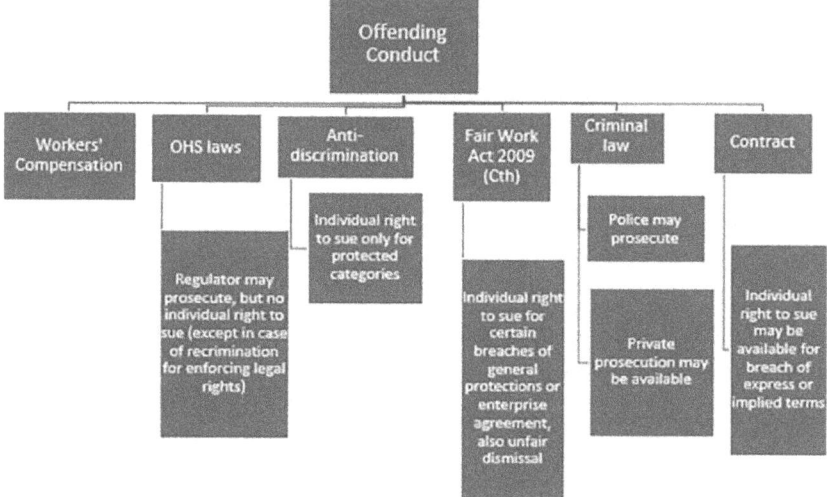

Figure adapted from Ryan Carlisle Thomas Solicitors, Submission 106

<u>Fair Work</u>

The Fair Work Commission (FWC) is Australia's national workplace relations tribunal. Most workers can apply to the FWC for an order to stop workplace psychological harassment; however, the FWC does not cover all Australian workers, such as those employed by local councils and state governments.

It is important to understand that the FWC anti-harassment jurisdiction is limited to preventing the worker from being bullied at work. It cannot issue fines or penalties and cannot award financial compensation. They focus on resolving the matter and enabling 'normal' working relationships to resume.

The FWC may make an order that a worker has been bullied at work. However, there remains a risk that the worker will continue to be bullied at work, taking into account internal procedures available to resolve grievances and disputes at the workers' workplace, final or interim outcomes arising from an investigation carried out by the worker's employer or other body, and any other matters the FWC considers relevant.

The Fair Work Act 2009 (Cth) (the Act) ss 789FC, 789FD, 789FF define bullying and the FWC's ability to make stop orders to stop bullying. Section 789FD provides that a worker is bullied if:

(1)   While at work in a constitutionally covered business.

(2)   An individual or group of individuals.

(3)   Repeatedly.

(4)   Behaves unreasonably towards the worker or a group of workers and

(5)   That behaviour creates a risk to the health and safety.

'Repeatedly' requires more than a one-off event, but there is no set number of harassment events; it 'might refer to a range of behaviours over time' that are different in nature. A risk to health and safety means the *possibility* of danger to health and safety and is not confined to actual danger to health and safety. The ordinary meaning of 'risk' is exposure to the *chance* of injury or loss. The risk must be real and not simply conceptual. A real possibility of danger needs to be identified. Some causal link must be demonstrated between the behaviour and the risk created. It need not be the only cause, but it must be a substantial cause ... 'viewed in a common-sense and practical way'.

The *Act* excludes 'reasonable management action carried out in a reasonable manner'. The unreasonableness of the behaviours is to be assessed objectively based on the circumstances. Unreasonable behaviour may include victimising, humiliating, intimidating or threatening behaviour, although it is not limited to that. The 'reasonableness' requirement is meant to be an objective assessment of the action in the context of the circumstances and knowledge of those involved at the time, with considerations including, for example, the circumstances leading to it, operating at the time and flowing from it. In addition, 'the specific 'attributes and circumstances' of the situation including the emotional state and psychological health of the worker involved may also be relevant'. Management action must be taken in a 'reasonable manner' considering facts and circumstances, such as how the action impacts the worker, circumstances and other relevant matters. The 'unreasonableness' must arise from the action, not the applicant's perception of it. Where there is a 'significant departure' by management from established policies or procedures, the reasonableness of that departure will be examined.

Emotionally abusive behaviour is not limited to verbal or physical abuse, but encompasses gestures, tone of voice, silence, and other acts or signs of exclusion or isolation, unwarranted criticism, unfair exclusion of a worker, or the imposition of meaningless tasks. A harassing environment can magnify other events or episodes that otherwise would be innocuous. Making deliberately false or vexatious claims, spreading rude and/or inaccurate rumours, or conducting an investigation unfairly or inappropriately can all constitute harassment. However, ordinary management action (for example, concerning performance monitoring) will not be regarded as harassment.

While the FWC must take into account any investigations already commenced by the employer, along with any relevant policies and procedures in place, the Act does not require the worker to utilise other options, such as requiring an employee to utilise internal resolution options or allowing an employer to finalise an ongoing investigation before it hears an application.

The FWC charges a modest fee, which can be waived in 'serious financial hardship' cases. The application is sent to the employer and the person alleged to be engaging in the behaviour; they have an opportunity to respond. The Commission deals with the application through mediation, conference, or hearing; it is resolved or determined by agreement between the parties, or the Commission may issue a decision or an order to stop the harassment.

The orders can include stopping their behaviour, regular monitoring and compliance with the employer's harassment policy. Fair Work can also require information, additional support and training and a review of the employer's harassment policy. Failure to comply can result in substantial penalties, but as noted above, the FWC cannot issue fines or award compensation.

For a worker to resort to the FWC means a process that they must pay for, and then they must submit to the investigation and complaints process just to get an order to stop the behaviour and be enabled to do their job without being bullied. This process does not contribute to the mental health of the victim, but instead costs the victim time and money, and again invests the victim in the process so they cannot move on and heal. Other than a 1-hour legal advice session that may be available, there is no assistance. The low number of cases submitted to the FWC suggests it has yet to become widely adopted as a solution for targets of harassment.

Fair Work General Protections contraventions

There is another avenue by which the Fair Work Commission (FWC) can deal with some harassment matters, and this may be available where there are alleged contraventions of the General Protections provisions. There are two main types:

1. Disputes - if a person has not been dismissed but alleges some other contravention of the general protections provisions, they may apply to the FWC to deal with the dispute.

2. Dismissals - if a person believes they have been dismissed and alleges that their dismissal contravenes the general protections provisions, they can apply to the FWC to deal with the dismissal. A general protections dismissal application must be lodged within 21 days of the dismissal taking effect.

Ideally, there are cases where the FWC is an excellent resource to help with unfair dismissal in the case of harassment, but again, targets should be aware of the realities of the process. The following submission summarises one person's experience of the process:

> *My submission for unfair dismissal due to termination of employment for exercising my workplace right in reporting workplace bullying simply resulted in a 90-minute phone conciliation of which an employer who has no desire to address the issue of bullying can simply plead ignorance and declare they have no authority to resolve the matter and therefore the matter goes no further. ... To this end fair work's handling of an unfair dismissal due to workplace bullying can simply be a waste of time as there is no compulsion to actually reach a resolution and no authority for fair work to take action even if it is clearly established that workplace bullying took place and the exercising of a workplace right in speaking up about it resulted in an employee's termination.*

Submission 15

Anti-Discrimination

While they are often related and the effects may be similar, harassment only falls under federal and state anti-discrimination legislation, where it can be proven that the harassment is linked to, or based on, one of the attributes covered by various federal anti-discrimination legislation. The specified attributes include:

- race (including colour, descent and national or ethnic origin).
- that a person is or has been an immigrant.
- sex.
- marital status.
- pregnancy or potential pregnancy.
- breastfeeding.
- family responsibilities.
- disability (including carers and associates); and
- age.

In cases where workplace harassment is based on any of these protected characteristics, victims may have recourse under anti-discrimination laws. The Australian Human Rights Commission and state-based anti-discrimination bodies can receive complaints and investigate instances of discriminatory behaviours. If a workplace harassment complaint based on discrimination cannot be resolved through mediation or conciliation, the bullied worker may commence court proceedings to seek a resolution. If a complaint is upheld, the court may order any remedy it sees fit, including, for example, ordering remedial action, an apology, monetary compensation or a combination of remedies. The employer can be held vicariously liable.

> *While the response from [the Australian Human Rights Organisation] was the most sincere, if the workplace bullying was not rooted in discriminatory behaviour, then their ability to respond is practically non-existent.*
>
> Submission 15

The recent introduction of the positive duty requirement under Section 47C of the Sex Discrimination Act 1984 (Cth) may help in addressing workplace psychological abuse. The positive duty mandates organizations to take 'reasonable and proportionate measures' to prevent sex-based discrimination in the workplace. Unlike previous mechanisms that relied on post-incident complaints, the positive duty emphasizes proactive measures before harm occurs. The potential for its influence beyond sexual harassment is partly due to the inclusion of 'related acts' and the guiding principles and standards. First, because the positive duty extends to 'related acts of victimization', it may be considered psychological harassment. Secondly, the four guiding principles - consultation, gender equality, intersectionality, person-centred and trauma-informed - along with the seven standards - leadership, culture, knowledge, risk management, support, reporting and response, and monitoring, evaluation and transparency - are to be implemented in all organisations. Both the standards and principles are elaborated upon extensively, and together, they could go a fair way toward stemming other forms of harassment. When embraced genuinely, the positive duty can help create safer, more inclusive work environments.

Work Health and Safety

Although there is no express prohibition on workplace psychological harassment in WHS laws, there is an implied duty on employers to protect workers from harassment. Everyone has the right to work in an environment free from harassment, discrimination and violence. Under the Occupational Health and Safety Acts, persons conducting a business or undertaking (*PCBUs*) have a legal responsibility to manage the health and safety risks associated with workplace bullying (defined as repeated, unreasonable behaviour directed at a worker or group of workers) and comply with any measures that promote health and safety in the workplace.

Under model workplace health and safety laws, a PCBU must eliminate or minimise psychosocial risks so far as is reasonably practicable. This can be done by following the risk management process: identifying the hazards, assessing the associated risks, implementing control measures to eliminate or minimise risks, and regularly reviewing control measures to ensure they remain effective. PCBUs must also consult workers about work health and safety and consult, cooperate and coordinate with other duty holders.

Psychosocial hazards include anything that could cause psychological harm (e.g. harm someone's mental health). Common psychosocial hazards at work include job demands, low job control, poor support, lack of role clarity, poor organisational change management, inadequate reward and recognition, poor organisational justice, traumatic events or material, remote or isolated work, poor physical environment, violence and aggression, bullying, harassment, including sexual and gender-based harassment, and conflict or poor workplace relationships and interactions. The *model WHS Regulations* require *PCBUs* to regard all relevant matters when determining what control measures to implement.

The Work Health and Safety Act 2011 (Cth) imposes a duty on 'a person' to eliminate risks to health and safety, so far as is reasonably practicable, and if this is not possible, to minimise those risks so far as reasonably practicable. 'Reasonably practicable' includes taking into account all relevant matters, including the likelihood of the hazard or risk occurring, the degree of harm that might result from the hazard or risk, what the person concerned knows or ought reasonably to know about the hazard or risk and ways of eliminating or minimizing the risk and the associated cost. Matters relating to hazards and risks include psychological hazards. Health means physical and psychological health. The Act provides for a primary duty of care for the health and safety of its workers:

'(1) A person conducting a business or undertaking must ensure, so far as is reasonably practicable, the health and safety of: (a) workers engaged, or caused to be engaged by the person; and (b) workers whose activities in carrying out work are influenced or directed by the person; while the workers are at work in the business or undertaking.'

Though only two States in Australia have a Code of Practice specifically for workplace harassment, Qld and Victoria, each state and territory has work health and safety laws and regulators that can investigate workplace psychological abuse complaints. Because of this duty, employers must eliminate or reduce the risks to employees' health and safety caused by workplace harassment.

The Australian House of Representatives Standing Committee on Education and Employment Inquiry into Workplace Bullying Final Report recommended that the Commonwealth Government, through Safe Work Australia, urgently progress, promote and implement the *Code of Practice: Managing the Risk of Workplace Bullying* and ensure it is embedded in workplaces, and several jurisdictions have updated their WHS laws to incorporate the Code.

WHS laws do not give injured workers, including bullied workers, any avenue to personally seek resolution outside of the workplace other than to make a complaint to their WHS regulator. Regulators can issue improvement notices or prosecute employers if they fail to address the issue. The criminal nature of the penalties and prosecutions under WHS laws means that the regulator must produce evidence strong enough to prove 'beyond reasonable doubt' that there has been a breach of duty by an employer or worker.

> *Worksafe: In my experience in having made a submission to Worksafe regarding workplace bullying, it was apparent that while Worksafe has a mandate to investigate workplace bullying, it only stretches as far as where criminal activity has taken place, where an employee has been physically injured in the course of workplace bullying.*
>
> Submission 15

An officer of an organisation may face liability if the organisation fails to meet its duty of care. The officer's duty recognises that certain individuals within organisations can influence the culture of the business or undertaking by ensuring that appropriate resources and processes to eliminate or minimise risks associated with harassment are adopted. Under all Australian WHS laws, workers are also required to take reasonable care when at work to avoid adversely affecting the health and safety of other people.

Workers' Compensation

If workplace harassment causes physical or psychological injury, victims may be eligible to make a workers' compensation claim. Each Australian state has its own legislation for workers' compensation. Generally, they provide benefits to employees who suffer a work-related injury or illness, including mental health issues resulting from workplace harassment. For example, the Workplace Health and Safety Queensland refers to 'Workplace Harassment' that endangers a worker's health, causing stress or any other physical harm, and employers can be found liable for not providing a safe place for their employees. Also, as Queensland has a code of practice specifically for workplace harassment, employees who reasonably believe they have been bullied in the workplace can apply to the Queensland

Industrial Relations Commission for an order to stop harassment. Success is not guaranteed.

> *I found that the Queensland workers' compensation system was geared to automatically reject any claims made on the basis of psychological injury due to workplace bullying.*
>
> Submission 34

Common Law Claims

Civil actions may be available under the law of tort and/or contract. In an action sounding in contract, because of the doctrine of privity, only the parties to a contract can sue under the contract. Therefore, it would be up to an employer to take action against a perpetrator of harassment in cases of breach of Codes of Conduct or breach of an enterprise agreement. Other employees, e.g. a target, cannot take action on this basis as they are not parties to that contract. However, there may be cases where a target might have a claim under the law of contract against the employer for breach of an express or implied contract term, for example, to ensure safe working conditions.

Defamation is a civil action sounding in tort (the law of civil wrongs) where there has been dissemination of information that has caused damage. Defamatory publications can come in the form of verbal statements, social media posts, emails, articles, podcasts, vlogs, blogs, text messages, radio and television shows, pictures, songs, and so on. For a publication to be defamatory, an ordinary person must view the material as likely to damage a person's reputation or, cause a person to be subjected to hatred, contempt, or ridicule, or to cause a person to be likely to be shunned or avoided. In the process of denigrating co-workers, it seems impugning a woman's virtue is alive and well. Whether a publication is defamatory is for a judge and jury to decide.

In some cases, victims of workplace psychological abuse may pursue common law claims for negligence and/or negligent or intentional infliction of emotional distress. Negligence claims typically involve proving that the employer failed in their duty of care or that the emotionally abusive behaviour amounted to intentional or reckless harm.

It is also worth noting that workers' compensation laws in some jurisdictions expressly restrict or prevent injured workers from suing their employer for damages under the common law. As a result, an employer may have less incentive to improve risk management and meet their WHS duties.

Criminal law statutes in each state and territory can apply to harassment. However, they are not uniform and may not serve enough of a deterrent to harassment behaviour if they are not enforced.

While acknowledging that coercive control occurs in other contexts, the state legislation criminalising aspects of coercive control currently only applies in intimate partner relationships.

Brodie's law is an amendment to the Victorian Crimes Act 1958; it makes serious bullying an offence punishable by up to 10 years imprisonment. The House Standing Committee on Education and Employment recommended that, through the Standing Council on Law and Justice, the Commonwealth Government:

- encourage all state and territory governments to coordinate and collaborate to ensure that their criminal laws are as extensive as Brodie's Law and

- encourage state and territory governments to consider greater enforcement of their criminal laws in cases of serious workplace harassment, regardless of whether work health and safety laws are being enforced.

Workplace psychological abuse in Australia: Summary of legal options

Fair Work Act	Anti-discrimination	Work health & safety (WHS)	Workers' compensation	Criminal law	Possible common law causes of action
-A target can apply to the Fair Work Commission if a covered Australian worker (not covered if the employer is a local or state government) -The focus is on resolution and enabling/re-establishing a normal working relationship. Generally, there are no fines or penalties and no financial compensation (but when there is a decision to stop the harassment, failure to comply can result in penalties -FWC will only make an order if satisfied that there has been harassment, and there is a risk it will continue -Target does not need to exhaust other options first, such as the employer's internal processes -A modest fee is assessed to file; a one-hour legal advice session is available -Often, there will be a mediation conference or hearing NB General protections provisions under Fair Work – two main types: Disputes Dismissals	-Applicable only if a protected class, and must be linked to one of the attributes covered under the legislation -The Australian Human Rights Commission and state-based anti-discrimination bodies receive complaints and investigate discriminatory behaviours. -If the matter cannot be resolved through mediation or conciliation, target can commence court proceedings, and the court can order any remedy, including remedial action, apology, monetary compensation, or a combination -Employers can be held vicariously liable	-Duty on employers to provide a safe workplace -Criminal penalties and prosecutions mean regulator must provide evidence of breach of duty by the employer or worker beyond reasonable doubt -Investigators can issue improvement notices or prosecute employers	-Workers compensation – state workplace, health and safety can seek orders to stop harassment -If a physical or psychological injury occurs, targets can make a worker's compensation claim – schemes vary across states and territories	-Brodie's law applies in Victoria	-Breach of contract against the employer for failure to ensure safe working conditions. -Negligent Infliction of emotional distress (intentional or negligent) -Defamation There is scant precedent; these common law avenues are generally not promising avenues unless it is an exceptional case and extensive resources of time, money, and emotional energy are available

Practical tips for targets contemplating legal action

Legal avenues might seem promising but less often deliver, as this submission highlights:

> *The costs of legal action for targets can be hugely significant, including:*
>
> *time and effort involved in preparation.*
>
> *financial expenses running into the tens of thousands of dollars.*
>
> *prolonged/exacerbated trauma.*
>
> *gagging clauses that prohibit targets from ever speaking about their experience or ever saying anything disparaging about their employer.*
>
> Submission 252

Other considerations, largely around the evidentiary burden, may render the pursuit of legal remedies less attractive:

- Complaints about workplace psychological harassment often do not fit the definition of harassment used by workplace regulators, making them difficult to prove.

- Harassment that is carried out deviously, subtly, and/or without witnesses, is harder to prove.

- It is nearly impossible to prove a negative, and very often workplace psychological harassment involves things that are not done, e.g. being ignored, not included in meetings and/or email distribution lists, not consulted about decisions, not mentioned for achievements, not asked to participate, not invited to group events, etc.

- Most complainants do not (and often cannot) provide enough detail in their complaint for it to be properly tested via an investigation. 'My supervisor regularly bullies me', for example, is not enough.

A Comparison of Potential Costs and Benefits of Legal Action

<u>The target MAY stand to gain</u>

- Financial compensation; however, in many jurisdictions there are statutory caps on awards.
- Some sense of vindication, perhaps.
- Being able to stay in the job.
- Some sense that the target stood up for themselves, but at what cost…?

<u>What legal action WILL cost the target</u>

- Financial costs, e.g. legal fees, court costs (potentially more significant in a 'loser pays' system).
- Time (that you could be spending on finding a new job, rebuilding, moving on, being happy!).
- Energy, mental and emotional - plus stamina (that you could be spending on finding a new job, rebuilding, moving on, being happy!).
    o Mental health – fighting a court case on this keeps you from moving on and healing, it keeps you in victim mode, reliving the trauma, and keeps you under scrutiny (blame the victim).
    o Plus it can be a source of real frustration, for example, as perpetrators are rewarded, promoted. Or if they are disciplined, may well end up on gardening leave, or getting paid out nicely thank you very much, while you fight on at great cost and get nothing.
- Confusion.

All the disadvantages notwithstanding, sometimes a legal action may be an appropriate choice, as it was for this person:

> *I had been told about the potential/inevitable stress any legal action would cause, and one psychologist, who had personally experienced workplace bullying herself, had recommended I just let it go. Nevertheless, I had made a personal resolution never to let anyone treat me like a doormat again after escaping a serious long-term domestic violence situation. I also wanted to change the fact that I had never stood up for myself, ever.*
>
> Submission 257

If the legal route seems like the right option, the target may wish to ensure they:

- Do their research and find out everything they can about harassment and the law related to it.

- Objectively evaluate the situation to ensure it really is harassment and how much they are likely to be able to change their circumstances, bearing in mind the overall situation.

- Determine the outcomes they realistically hope to achieve.

- Check their contract and enterprise agreement; knowing one's rights is the first step in protecting them.

- Check the job description - If they find their job changes after confronting the harassment and suddenly get menial tasks to do or are given an increased workload with shorter deadlines, which is not in their contract, they may be able to do something about it.

- Remember, every employer has a responsibility to provide a safe work environment. Check their employer's policy on harassment or unacceptable behaviour and read it thoroughly, making sure they understand the reporting procedure. When they decide to take action, they must follow the procedure for reporting harassment. Seek advice if it is ambiguous or unclear.

- State the facts clearly using their records as a chronology of what happened. Make sure it is in writing and follow the procedures.

- Keep a detailed record of every incident as each one happens, as they will need proof if they decide to make a complaint or take other action. The record needs to state who did and said what, the dates and times, list any witnesses, what actions were taken, and how they responded. This includes all the harassment incidents and anything that happened when they took action and involved their employers. Though time-consuming, this is vital. It is the evidence to prove their case and get listened to. They may have to prove that their employers failed to act or acted inappropriately after hearing about the problems.

- Try to get witnesses and ask them to record exactly what they witnessed as soon after the event as possible, including as much information as possible. Make sure that if they are asked to speak about it in a complaint or other situation, they will be prepared to do so.
- Seek advice and assistance from the union.
- Be realistic about resources for the long haul.
- Be mindful that it is not just the instant case that the employer cares about but also the prospective effect of a 'win' for the employee, which has the potential to spawn other claims. Individual targets need courage and a large dose of altruism to engage in what could be an even more scarifying experience than the impugned conduct itself.
- If they decide to leave their job because of the harassment, explain exactly why they are resigning and ensure they include the account of events in their resignation letter. This may prove useful in an unfair dismissal or general compensation claim. Be precise and factual, and do not just say they are leaving because they have been bullied.

Specific laws and procedures vary depending on the jurisdiction and circumstances of the case. Good legal advice will help to understand rights, options, and the processes involved in making a complaint or pursuing legal action. The billing rate of a good legal practitioner is typically several hundred dollars an hour, but no legal advice is better than bad legal advice. Unfortunately, a prospective client might be looking in the neighbourhood of anywhere between $500 and $5000 for preliminary advice, often to be told it is not worth pursuing anyway due to insufficient evidence, procedural problems, etc.

Top-tier firms are not only very expensive but are often conflicted out of representing employees because they focus on securing and maintaining the more lucrative employer representation. One option that may be useful is to find a good industrial relations practitioner. Some outstanding professionals in this field know the law well but cost significantly less than legal professionals. They can often guide a target well while saving them money, time and the frustration of protracted legal battles.

Prospects for law reform

The Australian House of Representatives Standing Committee on Education and Employment Inquiry into Workplace Bullying Final Report noted that, 'The current legislative and regulatory frameworks have created perceptions of an unfair and unjust system whereby only a minimal group of workers who have been bullied can seek individual recourse and remedies under anti-discrimination law, the *Fair Work Act* and workers' compensation law.' The Committee recommended that Government implement arrangements allowing an individual right of recourse for people targeted by workplace harassment to seek remedies through an adjudicative process. To date, no such individual right of recourse has been implemented.

> *There is a lack of investment by governments and funding bodies to support organisations and workplaces in understanding the damage caused by bullying more deeply. Equally, until organisations such as ours are supported through adequate funding arrangements, people experiencing bullying will receive limited help. The unintended consequence of this is that victims of bullying will continue to experience the devastating effects of the bullying long beyond the bullying.*
>
> Submission 57

We have become accustomed in many late-stage liberal democracies to look first to the government to fix things and increase government-level statutory protections. As in other areas, the government can encourage and discourage through incentives, resources, sanctions, etc.; in this way, the government has a role in facilitating change.

> *Workplace bullying is ...reinforced by the failure of governance and regulatory agencies to respond appropriately within their limited powers.*
>
> Submission 35

Fundamentally, however, because the underlying causes are cultural and systemic, we need more community awareness and action. The power lies with the community, with bystanders and leaders, with families and society, at the grassroots that flows up through and permeates every level.

Chapter conclusion

Litigation can quickly exhaust savings in addition to the emotional cost. It is time-consuming and isolating, and during this time the target has to stay invested; they cannot move on and heal. Some regulation does not permit an individual cause of action. Where it is permitted, individual complainants must carry the burden of proof, while often the entire managerial edifice colludes against them with greater resources and staying power. Also, the drawn-out process, dramatization and overreliance on punishment tend to reinforce victimhood. And, at the end of all this, targets are still likely to be out of a job.

Despite the disincentives, targets may feel that they cannot continue to tolerate the behaviour and must resort to legal action. They may hope to obtain financial compensation. They may feel compelled to stand up for their rights or reputation, and those of others. They want their employer to be more vigilant in preventing future occurrences. Whatever their reasons, evidence is key. Making this choice will be easier, and success more likely, for those who diligently and meticulously document the offending behaviours.

Selected references

Ballard, A., & Easteal, P. (2014). Mapping the legal remedy pathways for workplace bullying: A preliminary overview. *Alternative Law Journal, 39*(2), 94-98.

Branch, S., Ramsay, S., & Barker, M. (2013). Workplace bullying, mobbing and general harassment: A review. *International Journal of Management Reviews, 15*(3), 280-299.

Cobb, E. P. (2017). *Workplace bullying and harassment: New developments in international law.* Taylor & Francis.

Gewirtz, P. (1995). On I know it when I see it. *Yale LJ,* 105, 1023.

Keashly, L., & Harvey, S. (2006). Workplace emotional abuse.

The Prevention of Workplace Harassment Code of Practice 2004 (Qld).

Work Health and Safety Act 2011 (Cth).

https://digitalcommons.law.yale.edu/cgi/viewcontent.cgi?article=7665&context=ylj.

https://injury.findlaw.com/torts-and-personal-injuries/suing-for-emotional-distress-at-work.html.

https://www.austlii.edu.au/cgi-bin/viewdb/au/legis/cth/consol_act/fwa2009114/.

https://www.fairwork.gov.au/how-we-will-help/templates-and-guides/fact-sheets/rights-and-obligations/protections-at-work.

https://www.hcalawyers.com.au/blog/bullying-laws-around-the-world/#top.

https://www.hcalawyers.com.au/blog/bullying-laws-around-the-world/#top.

https://www.safeworkaustralia.gov.au/doc/model-code-practice-how-manage-work-health-and-safety-risks.

https://www.safeworkaustralia.gov.au/safety-topic/managing-health-and-safety/mental-health/psychosocial-hazards/poor-organisational-justice.

https://www.worksafe.qld.gov.au/laws-and-compliance/workplace-health-and-safety-laws/specific-obligations/health-safety-contact-centres/workplace-bullying.

Chapter Seven

The target's chrysalis – victim to victor

No one can make you feel inferior without your consent.
Eleanor Roosevelt

Chapter Introduction

And so we come to the return in our hero's journey. The initiation into the realities of workplace psychological harassment is a painful process, filled with dark nights and lessons we might well have wished we never needed to learn.

It isn't really accurate to say targets are the canaries in the coalmine, warning of toxic conditions. They might wish they could, but targets don't just get to keel over, and that's the end of them. They are, more often than not, the frontline crusaders, cannon fodder, who keep turning up daily, month after month, year after year. If there is any recognition and response to abuse, targets have to drive it. Standing up to harassment and shifting culture to a place where workers can thrive is essential work, but targets cannot force bystanders to participate and raise their voices in solidarity. They cannot force management to revise their power structures and approaches to worker interactions. Even when there is progress, it can be painfully slow. Change in the workplace will only come when there is real motivation and solidarity of purpose.

But alongside the struggle to improve our working world, there is another evolution taking place. Targets undergo an alchemy in the processes described in this book. Because we do have the power to change ourselves, as we seek to do our part to make a positive difference in the world.

Peter Drucker observed that one of the things commonly overlooked in a modern enterprise is the importance of managing oneself. Times of challenge present excellent opportunities to test and observe ourselves and learn more about who we are and how we can become our best selves.

We can welcome the opportunity to meet this challenge and to become transformed by the lessons of this difficult chapter in our lives. Hopefully, one day, every target can look back and say that they have learned from the experience and emerged stronger. This part of the book is about that. Offered here are a few personal observations and practical ideas and tools about surviving and growing through this time, as well as insights on prioritizing well-being, developing resilience, maintaining perspective and seeking professional support.

This chapter also canvasses the process of deciding to leave a toxic work environment, not as defeat but as a step in personal and career development. And it offers tips for starting over and finding work where you can be safe so that harassment does not happen again.

Staying strong

Prioritising well-being - Pathways to healing and resilience

Managing oneself includes taking care of one's well-being – physically, psychologically, emotionally and spiritually. There are many ways to do this with kindness and generosity. We can spend time with friends and family, and/or in recreation or meditation. We can check in with and be true to our values, and connect with gratitude and laughter.

Being a high-achiever has its rewards. At the same time, we should not feel constant pressure to prove our worth. It helps to be intentional and keep a balanced perspective about what we seek to achieve and what it means to us. There is pleasure in setting a goal and reaching it. But we also need to beware of our undervalued selves and forgive weaknesses and mistakes, our own and those of others.

Workplace psychological harassment can take an enormous toll on health and relationships. I knew how deeply I was personally impacted. However, I didn't understand how common this is and how serious the damage can be until I started researching and learning about what others have gone through. We need all the tools at hand to look after and protect ourselves. Tools and methods helpful in weathering and recovering from workplace trauma include:

- Establishing better boundaries to protect well-being, communicate needs assertively, say no when necessary, and create a work-life balance that prioritizes self-care and personal time.

- Self-care activities that promote physical, emotional, and mental well-being - exercise, yoga, meditation, journaling, spending time in nature, relaxation techniques, or pursuing hobbies and interests that bring joy.

- Support networks of trusted friends, family members, or support groups. Sharing experiences with others who have gone through similar situations can provide validation, understanding, and valuable insights.

- Accessing compassion as a healing agent, as Chekhov reminds us. Gabor Maté speaks of levels of compassion.

- Maintaining a healthy lifestyle by prioritizing nutrition, exercise, and adequate sleep. Taking care of physical health can positively impact mental well-being and aid recovery.

- Journaling to express thoughts, emotions, and experiences related to workplace trauma. It can be a therapeutic outlet for processing feelings and gaining insights into the recovery journey.

All of this is about resilience, the ability to emerge strong, healthy and successful after misfortune or disruptive change, prioritizing self-care and well-being, engaging in activities that promote physical health, mental well-being, and emotional balance, maintaining strong social connections and support networks; and seeking professional help when needed. It's about recovering from adversity, strengthening capacity to withstand and navigate difficult situations, maintaining a positive outlook and effectively coping with stress.

Resilience involves recognizing and understanding emotions and developing healthy coping mechanisms to handle them, remaining calm during challenging situations. It is also about finding solutions to problems and challenges, seeking alternative strategies and considering different perspectives. Resilient individuals tend to have an optimistic and positive outlook. Rather than dwelling on setbacks or negative circumstances, they focus on possibilities, and opportunities. They are flexible and adaptable, embracing a growth mindset. They can adjust their thinking, behaviours, and strategies in response to changing circumstances. They regard change as an opportunity for growth and learning rather than resisting or fearing it.

Seeking help – professional support for the physical, mental, emotional and spiritual well-being of targets

Health and other professionals can provide invaluable guidance and support. They can help with stress, anxiety, depression and their physical manifestations. Different individuals may respond better to certain therapeutic approaches and/or areas of focus, such as trauma. Mental health professionals can help determine the most appropriate tools and methods. They can provide many therapeutic interventions tailored to our specific circumstances and needs.

Faith-based and/or religious advice and support, values, philosophical counselling

To loosen our grip on the illusion of control takes a leap of faith, an antidote to the drought of faith that motivates power-seeking harassment and betrayal, not only by the perpetrator but by management and bystanders. Though I am not an expert in the varieties of religious experience, as I am not skilled in many of the areas dealt with in this short volume, I feel I have already presumed too much and will not venture into the powerful subject of faith. Gandhi titled the biography of his earlier years 'Experiments with the Truth'. By that, he said he meant 'looking for God'. Marianne Williamson is a voice among many who believe there is only one human problem: our separation from God. In this matter, I leave it there, noting that, for many, faith is their greatest - some might say their one and only - resource.

For some, in addition or as an alternative to faith, philosophical counselling can help to live in alignment with values. Socrates was one of the earliest proponents of philosophical counselling; the Socratic method of dialogue aimed to promote self-reflection and critical thinking. In modern times, Pierre Hadot emphasised the practical application of philosophy to address existential and ethical concerns and as a form of spiritual exercise. In the 1980s, Gerd B. Achenbach developed a system of philosophical counselling that integrated philosophical theories and practices with psychological insights. In recent years, Lou Marinoff, author of 'Plato, Not Prozac!', has popularised philosophical counselling and promoted the practice and training of philosophical counsellors.

Many of our problems arise from philosophical issues and dilemmas. We can be physically and psychologically healthy but face personal and existential challenges. Drawing on philosophical principles, values and ethics, philosophical reflection can provide clarity and practical solutions. A philosophical counsellor may employ Socratic questioning, thought experiments, and critical thinking techniques to facilitate exploration and self-discovery.

Many people find it useful to focus on connecting with values to help deal with harassment behaviours and even use this experience to become their best selves. Each of us decides every day and in various ways what values we prioritise in our lives.

There can be political expediency in touting values of kindness, transparency, and collaboration. Easy to talk about, such values are difficult, costly, time-consuming, easily perverted, and often perceived as threatening to power and control. Values are commodified and manipulated, and a good deal of posturing surrounds them. People and organisations can espouse certain values, but in fact embracing a different set, which is entirely opposed. It is easier at times to say that we believe in values than to live them.

The cardinal virtues of the Stoics can inform values. The Stoics teach that cultivating virtue is the path to a fulfilled life. Both necessary and sufficient for happiness, Stoics see virtue as the only good in our control. It ensures inner tranquillity and contentment, regardless of external circumstances. The Stoics identified four interconnected cardinal virtues: wisdom, courage, justice and temperance. They thought the best way to achieve inner tranquillity and contentment was to develop these virtues in harmony with nature and reason.

Humility, humour, gratitude and forgiveness

As an enabling value, humility provides a crucial part of the underlying substrate for all the others. Humility does not tell us what to do, but if we put humility in the equation first, the other values of kindness, courage, honesty, justice, and equality follow more easily. Humility is a great teacher, often spoken about, but frequently obscured by self-interest and promotion.

*Hu*mour is known to reduce pain and help with healing. Humour can be the key to defusing fear so that people connect instead of turning away. Even if it is risky, or maybe because it is, re-claiming the humour and even the joy of being together at work can accomplish two important things:

- Ameliorating the impact of abuse.
- Creating the team spirit, camaraderie, and solidarity that has been lacking - a lack that fuels escalating disharmony in the workplace.

An emphasis on the lighter side doesn't mean we don't take workplace psychological harassment seriously—quite the opposite. But we've supposedly taken it seriously for a long time, and things haven't changed. We have all heard Einstein's observation - the definition of insanity is doing the same thing and expecting a different result.

Gratitude allows us to connect with a greater appreciation for the positive aspects of our lives. We can shift our outlook by focusing on what we are grateful for rather than dwelling on what we wish were otherwise. Gratitude can be beneficial, too, in dealing with the discomfort of uncertainty by easing expectations, and taking the pressure off a bit. As noted throughout the earlier part of this book, uncertainty can be one of the challenging aspects of the process. Being grateful for what is and not having too many expectations helps us proactively shape our lives and outcomes through effort, perseverance, and personal growth.

Practising forgiveness is connected with humility, gratitude and humour. *Forgiveness, gratitude and humour are foundational to trust and institutional courage, discussed more in the next chapter.* Forgiveness is useful not only for fostering better relationships, but for a range of benefits for mental and emotional well-being:

- Forgiveness can help release negative emotions such as anger, resentment, and bitterness. Letting go of grudges and grievances allows us to heal emotionally and move forward.
- Forgiveness can alleviate the stress and anxiety of holding on to anger and resentment, promoting a greater sense of calm and inner peace.

- Forgiveness is crucial for repairing and strengthening relationships and can foster reconciliation, rebuild trust, and promote healthier communication and connection.

- Forgiveness can boost self-esteem. It reflects the ability to rise above pain, maintain values, and show compassion, which can enhance self-worth.

- Forgiveness involves cultivating empathy and understanding towards the person who has done the harm, seeing the situation from different perspectives and developing a deeper sense of compassion, which itself is healing.

- Research suggests that forgiveness is associated with reduced blood pressure, lowered heart rate, improved immune function, and a decreased risk of mental health issues like depression.

- Practising forgiveness supports resilience by encouraging self-reflection, learning from past experiences, and developing the ability to overcome adversity.

- By releasing grudges and letting go of the past, forgiveness can facilitate being more fully in the present moment, fostering happiness and contentment.

- Forgiveness can deepen spiritual connection, promote a sense of oneness, and support overall spiritual well-being.

Forgiveness does not necessarily mean condoning or forgetting the actions that caused harm. It is not reconciliation. Forgiveness means releasing the emotional burden and finding peace. It is as simple - and as challenging - as that.

Maintaining perspective

If we break a limb, one of the first things to do is take stress off the fracture. Similarly, when dealing with harassment, it's useful to reduce the stress of the situation. Engaging in disagreement and/or conflict can be mentally and emotionally exhausting. Sometimes, it can be best to keep a profile as low as possible.

By choosing which battles to fight, we conserve our energy for issues that truly matter or significantly impact our well-being. Not all conflicts carry equal weight or importance; attention and resources on the issues that align with our values, goals, and priorities will put them to best use.

'Pick our battles' does not mean avoiding all conflicts or staying silent in the face of injustice. It is about being intentional and thoughtful in choosing which battles to engage in, considering the potential impact, and finding the most effective ways to address concerns or resolve conflicts.

Selectively choosing when and where to engage in conflict is a strategic decision. Assess the potential outcomes, gauge the issue's importance, and determine the method, time, place, etc., to address it effectively. As Shakespeare's Polonius advised young Laertes, 'Beware of entrance to a quarrel, but being in, Bear't that the opposed may beware of thee.'

Conflict strains relationships; avoiding unnecessary disputes allows us to preserve relationships and find more constructive approaches. Picking our battles can contribute to well-being by reducing stress and promoting a more balanced and harmonious environment. It allows us to focus on positive aspects of life rather than being consumed by conflict.

Decision-making processes in difficult circumstances

The decisions a target is required to make in the context of workplace psychological harassment and the ensuing processes can be complex and confusing. The science of decision-making draws from psychology, economics, neuroscience, and other disciplines to explore human decision-making. Awareness of these processes can enhance clarity and lead to better-informed choices.

For example, bounded rationality recognises that individuals have limited cognitive capacity, time, and information when making decisions. People often rely on heuristics (mental shortcuts) and 'satisficing' (choosing an option that is 'good enough') rather than exhaustively analysing all available options. Cognitive biases are systematic patterns of deviation from rationality in decision-making due to information processing shortcuts. Bias, such as confirmation bias (favouring information that confirms existing beliefs) and anchoring bias (relying heavily on the first piece of information encountered), can lead to irrational decisions.

Our emotions provide valuable information to help us assess our feelings and preferences, shaping our choices. 'Positive' emotions, such as happiness or excitement, can enhance creativity and open-mindedness, leading us to seek rewards and take risks. 'Negative' emotions, such as fear or disgust, can make us more risk-averse. The 'affect heuristic' is reliance on emotion to evaluate objects, people, or situations, using emotional 'gut feelings' as a basis for decision-making rather than engaging in deliberate analysis.

Emotions can enhance decision-making or lead to irrational judgments if they override rational considerations. Understanding and managing emotions in decision-making can contribute to more balanced and effective choices. The relationship between emotion and decision-making varies depending on the context, individual differences, and cultural factors. Social factors, such as conformity, social norms, and peer pressure, can significantly impact decision-making. People often look to others for guidance, seek approval, or conform to group norms, which can influence their choices. Effective emotional regulation can help individuals make more rational and reasoned choices by mitigating the influence of others, and of impulsive or extreme emotions.

Befriending the Narrative

Befriending the narrative is about creating a relationship with how information about us is portrayed and perceived by others. Since pre-history, those who hold power have understood the importance of controlling the narrative. Consider how vital narratives are to ancient cultural traditions, and in an age of social media and spin, story matters.

To counter strategies and tactics like DARVO (Deny, Attack, and Reverse Victim and Offender) and outrage management, keep in mind that they rely on denial, devaluing the target, reframing the narrative, insistence on official channels and intimidation. Those who employ these tactics hijack the narrative, but we can:

- Counter denial by exposing the harassment with solid evidence.
- Counter devaluation by validating the target's positive traits.
- Counter reinterpretation and reframing by exposing the harassment as unfair and contrary explanations as wrong. (BTW, this

is tough stuff. If they are not honest, will we be? Will we remain true to our values?).

- Counter use of official channels by avoiding them and/or exposing their unfairness; and
- Counter intimidation and bribery by refusing and exposing them.

Befriending the narrative is not about manipulating or deceiving others but rather about actively shaping the perception of the story while respecting differing perspectives and remaining open to dialogue. Obviously, we cannot have complete control over how others interpret or respond to a narrative, but there are a few strategies to shape the narrative in a way that aligns with our perspectives:

- Proactively engage in shaping the narrative by taking the initiative to share perspectives, experiences, and achievements. Be proactive in communicating ideas, values, and goals.
- Develop a clear and consistent message that reflects the desired narrative. Clearly articulate values, and objectives concisely and compellingly.
- Be selective - strategically curate stories, examples, and anecdotes. Highlight positive experiences, successes, and instances where we have overcome challenges. Demonstrate our strengths, expertise, and positive impact.
- Utilize various communication channels to amplify the message and reach a wider audience. This can include written communication, social media, public speaking engagements, or engaging with relevant communities or networks.
- Cultivate relationships with people who can support and amplify the narrative. Seek allies, mentors, colleagues who can advocate for us and help reinforce the message. Collaborate with people who share similar values or objectives.
- Back up the narrative with evidence, data, and examples whenever possible. Use facts, statistics, testimonials, case studies to support claims and strengthen credibility.
- Acknowledge and address concerns or criticisms. Be open to feedback and demonstrate willingness to listen and engage in

constructive dialogue. Responding thoughtfully to concerns can help shape the narrative more positively.

- Maintain authenticity and transparency. Be genuine, honest, and ethical in presenting the narrative.

- Keep the narrative positive and strong. A great test of whether to speak up is asking – 'Does it need to be said? Does it need to be said now? And does it need to be said by me?' While letting loose with complaints and grievances may seem tempting, well-being does not thrive in an atmosphere of complaint. Connecting is hard when one is the perpetual bearer of bad news. Eventually, people start to tune out. So, while occasionally venting a little is perfectly human, it is helpful to aim also to embrace the lighter side.

- The research is clear - optimism is good for you. And it feels good, too. Maintaining and projecting a strong, positive, and values-driven attitude is a source of internal strength throughout this difficult process. It can help to alleviate and counter the stigmatisation and isolation targets must endure.

Intentional connection

Proximity, distance and boundaries

Another classic piece of advice worth remembering is 'keep enemies close.' While we may not like to think we have enemies, it is useful to be aware of who wants to help us, who may not be so supportive and who may even be quite willing to do us harm.

How we share information is important because information is a source of strength. Proximity can help prevent surprises or sudden escalations of conflicts. It also helps maintain control over the narrative and reputation, directly address false accusations or negative perceptions and counter attempts to undermine our credibility. Building bridges and finding common ground can lead to the possibility of transforming adversaries into allies or at least reducing hostility.

Being congenial with everyone facilitates observation and understanding. Building a relationship with an adversary affords the opportunity to gather information, better anticipate their actions and devise effective strategies. It may create opportunities to influence their opinions or decisions, change their perspective, seek compromise, or resolve conflicts more effectively.

Despite the potential benefits, keeping enemies close is a strategy that requires a level of emotional intelligence, discernment, and the ability to set personal boundaries. Sometimes, severing ties or maintaining distance may be a more appropriate approach to protect our well-being and preserve our values. It can be helpful to get distance from the workplace by spending time away, working from home when we can or taking leave. Distance removes us from the problem, helps us gain perspective, breaks the pattern, and gives us the space to reconnect with our own values and priorities. There may even be a chance to shift the perpetrator's focus. Humans are not entirely predictable, so none of this is an exact science. Often, it is trial and error. We also need to be flexible and agile.

'Right livelihood'

To be a person with integrity means to be whole and consistent in the working self and the rest of one's life, beliefs and values. Many philosophical and religious teachings require integrity in the sense of honesty and truth in all that we do. It matters how we turn up at work, what we do to make a living, what we produce, and how we behave in the marketplace, locally and globally.

For me, one important shift was my mindset around the purpose of working life; part of that was asking what was I doing the work for? Of course, we are paid to do a job, but how we do it and our purpose count. It is up to us to show up in a way that is true to ourselves. Otherwise, we may look back and regret that we were not true to ourselves. Self-betrayal can be harder to live with than losing.

To survive a toxic workplace, it can help to be *less* passionate about work. As with any relationship, it can ease the pressure not to freight working relationships, including the relationship with work itself, with more than they can bear. The place of work in our lives is a choice. To have both lucrative and fulfilling work is not guaranteed, but it is worth aspiring to.

Expectations and boundaries

The ambiguity of unclear roles invites the sort of discretion that fuels harassment. Subjectivity and uncertainty leave the door open to abuse, so it is important to be clear about expectations. The vaguer the job roles are, the sketchier the parameters are, and the more likely harassment can occur. Confusion over values, objectives and roles lies at the heart of many problems in the modern work environment.

Establishing clear boundaries at work helps define roles, responsibilities, and expectations, setting the parameters for acceptable and unacceptable behaviour and working together effectively. Well-defined boundaries can improve productivity and focus by removing unnecessary distractions or interruptions and facilitating better time management and task prioritization. Boundaries help prevent unwarranted intrusions and related conflicts and create a sense of safety. They can also help uphold professional standards and clear personal or ethical lines. Finally, boundaries can help preserve work-life balance, keeping personal time, family commitments, and self-care respected and protected.

The slightest expressions can be used against us, and things become amplified as they make the rounds. We are wise to be circumspect about sharing information. Also, teasing or joking could be taken the wrong way. Keeping our communications simple, positive, courteous, collegial and respectful is the safest policy. Only say what needs to be said. No innuendo, no editorialising.

Coping with isolation

The dynamic of harassment and its denouement is designed to isolate the target. Isolation is painful and can be very damaging. Links between social isolation and serious medical conditions are not fully understood, but ample evidence supports the connection.

However you look at it, isolation can be challenging, and because of this, in the context of harassment, it is useful to cultivate one's networks. Sometimes we all need to unburden ourselves, especially with professionals, friends, family, mentors or others outside of work. There is a world of people who can help. Seeking help, whether professional or otherwise, can be a positive step not only for its own sake but also for the very act of doing so, which reduces the sense of isolation and helplessness.

Consider who can be of assistance and in what ways. Consider carefully the whom you can trust, what support and assistance they can provide, and be realistic about how that looks and the benefits and risks of seeking help. Often, the roles of people who support us can become confused, so it is important to be sensitive and communicate well and appropriately with each of them. Hopefully, they will do the same for you and be generous and forgiving.

Some advice about workplace issues suggests that support might come from our manager (if not themselves the perpetrator), co-workers (ditto), other colleagues, a mentor or a coach; someone in HR/P&C or senior management (if there is anyone there we can trust), our union; the Employee Assistance Program (EAP); a medical practitioner or a mental health professional; a spiritual advisor; our family and friends, our partner; a legal representative; Fair Work; the Australian Human Rights Commission; State or Territory agencies including Workplace Health & Safety. My advice is to be extremely careful about trusting anyone connected with the workplace, including union officials, though some have a positive experience of support through their union, as the following submission indicates:

> *... the response of this union and I believe unions in general was very proactive. ... the union's willingness to look objectively at a case and if it saw merit ... make their members aware of the bullying.*
>
> Submission 15

Outward focus: Healthy competition and collaboration

> *I can only hope that my experience will serve to stop this cancer that has spread across our society almost unnoticed, almost ignored, almost accepted. I am more than happy to contribute and actively work towards workplaces free of this illness. I have lived through hell - and I would not wish anyone in this world to go through it.*
>
> Submission 281

There is a positive synergy possible between collaboration and competition when we push each other to achieve, celebrating and encouraging the best in each other rather than putting others down or worse. If we are not successful in a certain task or role, we can accept that it wasn't meant for us, but we can also engender enthusiasm among colleagues to do the work of finding the optimum path for each of us and achieving our best together, not just as individuals.

> *There are others who have not been blessed with as much support as I have. So, I look for ways to help. That is a gift to be grateful for.*
>
> Personal diary

Cutting the cord

The writing on the wall

The main themes of this book have to do with changing the workplace culture to minimise workplace psychological abuse and the collective courage that is essential to any real progress. Workplace psychological harassment is everybody's business. Everyone in the workplace, from the CEO to the most junior new hire, should be encouraged to develop and support dignity at work. Until that happens, however, the burden of confronting harassment is on targets. However far targets engage with the challenge of overcoming psychological harassment, at some point, most grapple with the difficult decision whether to walk away.

If the organisation does not have an interest in change, in genuinely preventing and stopping harassment, staying in the job is like staying in an abusive relationship. A target can try to stand up to the harassment and work through the processes, but they cannot stop the perpetrator without assistance. Ultimately, things will not change until the organisation wants them to and starts putting the pieces in place for reform. This brings us back to where we started this book - the right to a safe workplace. Until the employer takes responsibility for making that happen, the best choice may be to look elsewhere for a safe work environment.

Sixty to seventy per cent of targets of harassment leave their jobs. Leaving is not easy. It takes effort, energy, optimism, enthusiasm, and the type of strength that a target worn down by harassment may struggle to access. There comes a time, however, sooner or later, when many targets, frustrated and discouraged, decide they must leave.

Whether and when it is time to leave depends on the circumstances. How long can we hang in, what are the risks and rewards, and how much can we take on if we stay and fight against the emotionally abusive behaviour and culture? Targets base their choice of strategy on three criteria: desire to remain with the organisation, degree of perceived congruence between their attitudes and beliefs and those of the supervisor and perceived protection from arbitrary actions by the perpetrator. Eventually, it becomes clear to the majority of targets that they must walk away. Usually, looking back, we wish we had done it sooner. But this is where planning and advice, mindfulness, self-care and being intentional about the situation are very useful.

Winning, losing, leaving

Walking away does not mean losing. The fact is, the consequences of any set of events cannot be known with certainty. Winning and losing are freighted concepts. Each of us must decide what success looks like, depending on our own unique goals, values, and aspirations.

Aligning actions and achievements with our core values is crucial to feeling successful and accomplished as unique individuals. Success may mean financial stability, material possessions or attaining certain career milestones and/or it may be about service, positively impacting society or meaningful connections with loved ones.

Sometimes, it feels like we are getting knocked down repeatedly, but it helps to see value in accepting and learning from what can feel like loss, and so develop essential life skills like problem-solving, adaptability, and perseverance. We can also develop qualities in ourselves that are meaningful and valuable for the rest of our lives, like humility.

> *There was a movement a few years ago for people to meet up and talk about and celebrate failure, but it seems to have failed.*
> Personal diary

Every situation can be a catalyst for growth that can ultimately lead to greater success (as we define it) in the long run. Accepting setbacks can help us cultivate a realistic perspective on our abilities and limitations. We can recognise that success is not guaranteed and that hard work and continuous improvement are necessary for achieving the goals we set for ourselves. This perspective can foster a sense of gratitude, empathy, and a willingness to learn from others. Resilience, determination, and a positive attitude in the face of defeat can be a testament to character and inspiring others. And if revenge is your thing, what can be better than to emerge stronger and better from these events?

Exit strategy

An exit strategy is unique for each of us, based on our individual circumstances and career goals. Planning and executing the exit strategy professionally and respectfully maintains positive relationships. Keeping our purpose and values at the forefront of everything we do can help us grow our potential and limit the chance of regrets down the track. In planning an exit strategy, we may wish to:

- Review our finances - consider how long we can sustain ourselves financially without a steady income. Set up a rainy-day fund to support us during the transition period between jobs.

- Take time to reflect on our past experiences and learn from them. Assess what we enjoyed and what we would like to avoid in future roles. We can use this insight to make informed decisions and set ourselves up for success in our new job.

- Evaluate our current job satisfaction, career goals, and reasons for wanting to leave. Reflect on what we want to achieve in our next professional endeavour and ensure it aligns with our long-term aspirations.

- Develop a job search strategy. Determine how to allocate time for searching, networking, and applying to positions. Set goals, establish a timeline, and track our progress to stay focused and organized.

- Cultivate and expand our professional network. Attend industry events, join relevant associations or groups, and approach contacts in our field. Networking can help us uncover new job opportunities and gain valuable insights and advice.

- Research potential job opportunities, companies, and industries that interest you. Consider company culture, growth prospects, and alignment with our values.

- Explore options through online job boards, company websites, and professional networks.

- Identify our strengths and any skill gaps that may hinder our job search. Consider taking courses, attending workshops, or gaining certifications to enhance our qualifications and marketability.
- Polish the resume and update the LinkedIn profile to reflect recent achievements, highlighting strengths and accomplishments.
- Practice interviewing techniques and prepare responses to interview questions. Do some research so you can demonstrate knowledge and enthusiasm during interviews.
- Contact references in advance.
- Once we secure a new job offer, decide how and when to give notice to our current employer. Consider contractual requirements, including notice. Maintain a positive attitude during the transition period and offer assistance with the handover process.

Better to resign or be terminated?

When there is no choice but to leave, whether 'tis nobler to resign… or is it better if the employer terminates? We may not have the choice, but if we do, the decision to resign or be terminated depends on personal circumstances, career goals, and the specific situation at hand.

It can be better for our reputation if we resign, so it appears that we took the initiative to make a voluntary decision. This can be important when seeking future employment. Resigning may enhance the possibility of negotiating severance and a positive recommendation. It may also afford greater control over when and how we leave the job and facilitate planning our transition. Perhaps most importantly, if we are in a toxic or unhealthy work environment, resigning can provide us with a sense of relief and the opportunity to prioritize our mental and emotional well-being.

Financially, in some circumstances it may be advantageous to wait for the employer to terminate. If we are terminated, as long as it is not for misconduct, we will probably retain the right to claim unemployment compensation. In some cases, termination may entitle us to receive a severance package, unemployment and/ or other benefits, depending on our employment contract and/or relevant labour laws. This financial support can keep us afloat during our job search or transition period. Be warned, however, the current regulatory environment makes it difficult for employers to terminate, and very often, they can wait us out or force us out by creating performance management issues or even manufacturing claims of harassment against us.

In some situations, a target may feel forced to resign. Under these circumstances they may still have grounds to make an unfair dismissal claim (subject to eligibility criteria) based on 'constructive dismissal', that the employee had no alternative but to resign due to the employer's actions.

There are also situations where an employer may agree to treat a termination as a resignation conditional upon the employee agreeing to release the employer from any future claims concerning their employment and the termination, including unfair dismissal claims or unlawful termination claims. Such an agreement is recorded in a 'Deed of Release' that the employer can later rely upon as a bar to any future claims made by the employee.

Ultimately, deciding between resigning or being terminated depends on the circumstances, long-term career goals, financial situation, emotional well-being, and the potential impact on professional reputation. Due to the complexities of various legal actions that may be available, it is best to consult a legal and/or industrial relations professional with expertise in this area for guidance appropriate to the specific situation and applicable law.

<u>Never a next time- Due diligence for the next job</u>

Perhaps the most important thing that targets (and all workers as potential targets) can do is to make sure it never happens again, stopping harassment before it starts, so there isn't a next time. The sad fact is that people can and do end up being targets of harassment more than once. There are ways we can make better choices about where and with whom we work so that people who are harassed do not get harassed again.

Sometimes, financial circumstances require us to take a job, whatever job we can find. But most of us, to some extent, have a choice about what jobs we take. In making that choice, we have a right to ask prospective employers whether they will provide a safe work environment.

Find out who we will report to before we take the job. Talk to that person, and, if possible, talk to some people who report to that person. Because the adage is true - people join organisations, but *they leave managers*. It can only help to discern as much as possible what position we will occupy in the complex interrelationships of organisational and workplace politics.

Before taking a new job, we can find out as much as we can about the workplace culture and the people we will be working with to ensure this is a workplace where we have a high chance of success. Before we accept a job, find out - does the workplace practice safe work hygiene? Will we be supported? Do they do the good things that they say they do? Are workers free to speak about their experiences and workplace conditions? It is not always easy to tell because employers want to create a positive image, and many workers are not free to speak out. Aware of this, we can look for the signs. And if we have periods of probation, so do they. Not every work relationship is a good fit. There are many good reasons to keep our professional networks current; an important one is that we may need to leave again. Because one thing we know with certainty is that workplace psychological harassment is not a rare occurrence.

There are questions we would do well to ask. Yes, humans have an optimism bias - this job will be great! But we can temper that optimism with some research and balance it with a realistic assessment of what we're actually signing up for.

To prevent and stop workplace psychological harassment, we must first understand what we are looking for - and looking out for. Ensure the organisation we will work for is genuinely committed to values, culture, policies and practices that prevent and stop harassment for our well-being and that of our family and loved ones. An example of an AI tool recently developed to help with this research is Culturama, which covers over 30 industries and, as of this writing, includes 1750 global organisations. Based on an automated analysis of over 6 million employees' natural language opinions, the product collects information on work-related problems to help employees make informed career decisions. Hopefully, in the future, we will have more tools to help hold organisations accountable and improve working conditions for everyone.

Chapter conclusion

To be a victim is not to become one. While some targets are irrevocably damaged, the aim is to emerge stronger. The first step is to acknowledge the impact. Denying or avoiding this reality can exacerbate the situation and/or prolong its negative effects. Acceptance brings awareness and clarity; it is the starting point for seeking help and finding solutions. Acceptance shifts crucial energy from denial to problem-solving and decision-making, and it can minimize further damage or consequences.

Victimhood is real and deserves empathy, understanding, and recognition of the complexities of individual experiences. A victim mindset can lead to feelings of helplessness, hopelessness, and a lack of control. It perpetuates a cycle of negativity that prevents people from moving forward. It is easy to see how victimisation can even beget perpetration, given that pressure to perform with limited support and resourcing is a common cause of harassment.

The good news is that crises can lead us to rebuild our lives for the better. The experience may involve uncertainty, distress, trauma and emotional breakdown as we grapple with the processes of growth, self-understanding and self-development. During a breakdown, we may wonder whether we have gone mad, but our agitation obscures a logical search for health. 'We haven't become ill; we were ill already. Our crisis, if we can get through it, belongs, in the most acute way, to the search for self-knowledge.'

The challenge is not letting the experience of being a target diminish one's agency and strength. People who have experienced victimization can demonstrate resilience and strive for healing, justice, and empowerment. Targets may find it helpful to avoid adopting the victim mentality consciously. Rather than blaming others or external factors, they can instead focus on improving their situation, taking responsibility for their actions and choices. A mindset of growth and empowerment fosters a sense of resilience and personal agency that contribute to improved psychological well-being.

Successfully navigating any crisis can be a transformative experience. Dealing with psychological harassment is potentially transformative. So often profoundly damaging, there is no question that this is a dangerous time. Nevertheless, it can also be a chrysalis for targets, from which we can emerge stronger, wiser and better equipped for the next chapter, whether it is in the current workplace or, as is more likely, something new.

Selected references

Fraser, J. (2022). *The bullied brain: Heal your scars and restore your health*. Rowman & Littlefield.

Kahneman, D., & Tversky, A. (1982). The psychology of preferences. *Scientific American*, 246(1), 160-173.

McDonald, Mary Catherine (2023). *Unbroken: The trauma response is never wrong: And other things you need to know to take back your life*. Sounds True.

Mills, C. B., Keller, M., Chilcutt, A., & Nelson, M. D. (2019). No laughing matter: Workplace bullying, humor orientation, and leadership styles. *Workplace health & safety*, 67(4), 159-167.

Real, T. (2022). *Us: Getting Past You and Me to Build a More Loving Relationship*. Rodale.

Sharpe, M. (2022). *Stoicism, Bullying and Beyond: How to Keep our Head When Others around You Are Losing Theirs and Blame You*, Balboa Press.

Zhou, R., & Lu, H. (2022). The 4Rs approach to COVID-19 emergency management during the post-pandemic period: What lessons can be learned from Shenzhen, China? *Infectious Medicine*, 1(4), 272-275.

https://commonslibrary.org/backfire-manual-tactics-against-injustice/.

https://culturama.is/#/home/main.

https://iconreputation.com.au/manage-reputation-crisis-ebook.

https://www.curioussoulphilosophy.com/what-is-philosophical-counselling.html.

https://www.researchgate.net/profile/Jose_Navarro12/publication/256466911_Modeling_workplace_bullying_using_catastrophe_theory/links/547e14340cf2c1e3d2dc1920.pdf.

https://alchemycoaching.life/podcasts.

Chapter Eight

Transforming workplace psychological abuse

If you don't choose to do it in leadership time upfront, you do it in crisis management time down the road.

Stephen Covey

Chapter Introduction

Self-help strategies for individuals, such as those touched upon in the previous chapter, are available - indeed essential - anytime. However, it is wrong to permit self-help to deflect the responsibility for this shared malaise that pervades organisations. It is yet another instance of evading accountability that fuels the problem. In many ways, it IS the problem.

Acknowledging that it may be essential to individual well-being, self-help can never fix what is, at its core, a social issue. Workplace psychological harassment is a social problem for which any enduring solution has to be a collective effort. But, given that management, colleagues and other bystanders look the other way, the task of stopping workplace psychological harassment rests with targets, who are rarely in the best position to do so. The complaints process typically plays out in ways unfavourable to the target. Legal processes outside the organisation also come with heavy costs and risks and are rarely favourable to targets.

This chapter describes a more effective and enduring crisis management approach as an alternative to the standard burden-and-blame the victim. It outlines steps for organisations to comply with their legal and moral responsibilities through comprehensive policies and procedures for recognising, responding to, and remedying psychological harassment at the institutional level. Further, this Chapter advocates for a shift from a complaints culture and conflict mindset to a relationship management culture, encouraging bystander and leadership courage in fostering a safe and healthy work environment. Because workplace psychological harassment is a social, institutional and political problem, it is up to all of us to connect with the courage to change it together.

Recognition

Transforming a workplace from one that breeds harassment to one that is healthy and safe requires clarity on what harassment is and what behaviours will not be tolerated. We have seen that, as distinct from sexual harassment and egregious physical violence, workplace psychological harassment is notoriously difficult to define; this is part of what makes it so easy to turn away from and ignore. And, Potter Stewart notwithstanding, we are less likely to recognise it when we do not know what it is.

As noted in Chapter Two, what workplace psychological harassment is (and is not) is very much about what is agreed at any given place and time. This agreement/shared understanding forms the basis on which rules and processes can be structured. So, the first step for genuine recognition is awareness and understanding at the collective level. This social issue must be dealt with as a social problem, not an individual psychological problem or a problem that can be independently dealt with separately through legal channels without this collective understanding. Through concerted action, we need to arrive collectively at a guiding framework to prevent and stop harassment developed through a shared understanding of what we are seeking to curtail, balancing the interests of good management, transparency, collaboration, innovation, etc. Currently, the lack of clarity around what is and is not workplace psychological harassment is problematic, and it fuels excuses to ignore the problem.

Recognition is also about breaking the silence, spreading awareness, ending the dance of denial and acknowledging the reality of the conditions that lead to harassment. It requires management to shift from the guiding principle that 'Even a bad manager is better than a whistleblower. An employee who speaks about harassment in the workplace threatens the status quo, incumbent power structures and reputational capital, and therefore is not one of us.' It means adopting a new ethos that says, 'We value communication from all workers. An employee who speaks about harassment in the workplace is a sentinel who provides a valued service. We welcome every opportunity to improve as a healthy, safe learning organisation. Our own reputational capital and the organisation's will be stronger for it.'

In a safe learning organisation, speaking up is encouraged. The organisation builds awareness, implements education and training, and cultivates communication and transparency (e.g. through disclosure, 360-degree reviews, surveys, listening, and witnessing). While the individual's privacy must be respected, aggregate data, policies and processes should be open to public input and scrutiny, thwarting harassing behaviours that thrive in secrecy.

Valuing the truth and transparency means valuing the people who report their experiences. It requires organisations to stop blaming targets for reporting and instead value them as the truth-tellers who serve a crucial role by preventing harm, exposing wrongdoing, promoting accountability, shedding light on unethical practices, helping deter future misconduct and creating impetus for industry improvements.

According to the concept of 'Exit, Voice, Loyalty', when an organisation demonstrates a decrease in quality or benefit, stakeholders can exit (withdraw from the relationship) or use voice (attempt to repair or improve things through communication). Exit, taken alone, provides the warning sign. Voice provides reasons. The greater the availability of exit, the less likely voice will be used. However, loyalty affects the choice between exit or voice. Where there is loyalty to the organisation, voice is more likely, and exit may be reduced. Because voice implies loyalty, management should value it and repay it by looking after those who take on the burden of speaking up. Loyal stakeholders become especially devoted to the organisation's success when their voices are heard, their concerns are recognised, and there is genuine response.

Ideally, the courage of loyal employees, who stay and use their voice, fosters ethical behaviour, inspires others, and establishes a culture of integrity. By valuing these workers, organisations send a message that courage and willingness to come forward are respected and protected. While an employer may not be able to stop all retaliation toward those who speak up, it can reward courage, commitment and loyalty with supportive reporting mechanisms, legal protections and real value placed on honesty, integrity and accountability.

Response

Recognition is a critical first step, but recognition alone is insufficient, unless there is effective response. We have seen that management often avoids accountability in the recognition stage by discouraging speaking up and at the response stage by making complaints difficult, by siding with perpetrators and adding to the victimisation of targets in the process of compounded betrayal. The guiding principle, 'A problem not recognised or responded to is not a problem,' must be replaced with a new guiding framework that says, 'Building a better organisation matters to us. We recognise **and respond** through genuine, effective policies and procedures.'

This means employers provide genuine effective assistance and support to victims of psychological harassment, that they dispense with the charade of response that actually undermines and obstructs, as discussed in Chapter Five. Employers must ensure procedural justice and safe work environments when provided with evidence.

Organisations need appropriate learning and development programs to safeguard against workplace psychological harassment, putting policies, procedures, and systems in place for identifying the psycho-social safely risks and ensuring these are appropriately managed. Inadequate or ineffective policies, processes and procedures correlate with higher rates of workplace psychological harassment. From a prophylactic and compliance perspective, all organisations must have an anti-harassment policy with complaints and investigation procedures - and ensure staff implement it. From a compliance perspective, failure to implement these policies could make a business more susceptible to a Fair Work, anti-discrimination, WHS or other legal claim.

Transforming complaints culture

Where there is friction in an organisation, management can ignore and suppress the issue, or recognise it for what it is and respond productively. Managed appropriately, diversity of views is essential to organisational growth, and effective communication and feedback develops healthy structures. Real respect for diversity is a sign of a healthy institution.

It is vital to comprehend that psychological harassment is qualitatively different from conflict and dispel the myth of the dyadic dodge discussed in Chapter Three, including the idea that there is a shared interest in resolution. Conflict resolution approaches applied to harassment need to be structured appropriately. Harassment can only be resolved effectively and adequately through processes suited to its particular nature and dynamics and carried out by skilled professionals.

Addressing the shortcomings of the complaints process for workplace psychological harassment requires organisations to prioritize creating a safe reporting environment, conducting thorough investigations, providing timely updates, and implementing appropriate remedial actions. In addition, it is important to find ways to incorporate proper justice and relationship management processes.

The modern workplace runs on relationships. Promoting open communication, fostering respect, and enforcing consequences for inappropriate behaviour support the effective function of those relationships.

We know complaint processes are often more damaging than harassment and can actually exacerbate the trauma. Effective processes would treat targets as loyal employees, fulfilling a beneficial function as a species of internal consultant, acting in concert with and in the organisation's best interests. When isolated and blamed for breaking the code of silence, targets become frustrated and worn down by inappropriate, ineffectual and perverse processes. When the process becomes antagonistic, they pursue their own interests of self-preservation, and their actions are unlikely to lead to the best outcomes for their team, the organisation or for themselves.

Complaints processes that continue to isolate targets and frustrate genuine response and transformation need rethinking and revision. This is one of the many reasons collective response is urgently needed. In isolation, targets cannot effect the needed transformation of workplace culture, including complaints culture. It takes all of us together, accepting responsibility in a spirit of positive change and transformation to improve policies and procedures in the interests of safe workplace culture.

Putting in place better policies, practices, and procedures

Strong policies, practices, and procedures for protecting workers' health and safety discourage psychological harassment. They minimize and/or remove the conducive conditions (e.g. frustration, perceived power imbalances), motivating structures (e.g. reward systems, internal competition and inordinate emphasis on the isolated concept of leadership), and precipitating processes (e.g. organisational change, downsizing) discussed in Chapter Four.

A safe and respectful work environment has clear anti-harassment policies and actively supports employees who come forward. Management's evidence of commitment to addressing harassment sets the tone for more effective complaints processes.

The Australian government advises that workplace harassment policies (whether formal or informal) should include the following:

- a definition of workplace harassment with examples.
- the process for reporting workplace bullying and encouraging workers to use the process (recognise, respond, remediate).
- accountability and responsibilities of categories of staff, i.e. who makes the decisions.
- contact points within the organisation if a person has questions.
- the investigation process - where necessary.
- the process for managing vexatious reports.
- the consequences for not complying with the policy.

The policy should also include standards for behaviour or conduct, designated reasonable time frames for various stages of a complaint process, a description of complaint procedures and the nature of the investigative process, and systems for monitoring, recording, and internally publicising complaints and their outcomes, adhering to principles of due process and natural justice.

HR/P&C departments have a significant, complex and multi-dimensional role in organisations. Part of that role is to make it safe for employees to call out harassing and other unsafe behaviours. HR/P&C departments and personnel can be oriented to recognise toxic leadership, understand its effects, and provide counsel to employees affected by toxic leaders.

Organisations can monitor the health of their own complaints processes through checklists that cover a range of questions.

These include:

Questions about policy and culture, such as:

- Does the organisation make stopping harassment an organisation-wide priority, where everyone is accountable?

- Does the organisation co-design, implement and communicate clear policies that explicitly define workplace psychological harassment, the consequences for engaging in such behaviour, and the reporting mechanisms available to employees? And does it ensure that these policies are easily accessible to all employees?

Questions about the process, such as:

- Does the organisation offer safe, confidential reporting and response procedures, including gathering relevant evidence, interviewing all parties involved, and ensuring impartiality that encourages employees to report incidents of harassment without fear of retaliation? Are there multiple reporting channels, such as anonymous hotlines, reporting platforms or designated individuals, that can provide alternative avenues to ensure employees feel comfortable coming forward?

- Does the organisation keep records, such as harassment reports, conversations, meetings and interviews? Does it have a mechanism to ensure that records are unbiased and accurate?

- If the organisation decides that a report needs further investigation, does it inform the target of the additional investigation process?

- Does the organisation treat all reports seriously and respond quickly and reasonably following policies and procedures? Does it respond sensitively to target disclosures? Has it created a trauma-informed reporting policy?

- Does the organisation avoid the dance of denial? Does it avoid the DARVO's institutional betrayal practice?

- Is the organisation cognisant that even some well-intentioned responses can be harmful, for instance, by taking control from the target or minimizing the harm? Does it educate, train and cultivate better listening skills to respond sensitively? Does it integrate the understanding that workplace psychological harassment is not the same thing as conflict?

- Instead of delay, non-responsiveness, and outrage management, does the organisation conduct prompt and thorough investigations into harassment complaints? Has the organisation ended the tactics engineered to produce the result that the target quits or is silenced?

Questions about communication, and mediation and investigation processes such as:

- During the process - Does the organisation keep relevant employees informed of the process and estimated timeframes, and explain reasons for delays?
- Related to process - Does the organisation create ways for individuals to discuss what happened to them, accept accountability and apologise where appropriate?
- Does the organisation ensure prompt, thorough, fair and unbiased processes for mediation and investigation, including ensuring that external personnel are suitably skilled, neutral parties?
- Related to outcomes - Does the organisation communicate the outcome, actions taken, the reasons for decisions made and any right of review if the parties are not satisfied with the outcome?

Questions about remediation, such as:

- If psychological harassment is substantiated, does the organisation attempt to resolve the matter and take appropriate remedial actions to address the issue? Does it hold accountable those who engage in harassing behaviour, regardless of their position or tenure, ensuring there are consequences?
- Does the organisation guard against the risk management mindset and stretch beyond minimum standards while striving for excellence in non-violence and equity?
- Does the organisation comply with criminal laws and civil rights codes and go beyond mere compliance, avoiding a checkbox approach?

Questions about support, such as:

- Does the organisation combat the isolation and stigmatisation of employees who report harassment? Does it support, assist and rehabilitate, rather than blame the target, ending the narrative that 'the target is the problem'?
- Does the organisation offer genuine, comprehensive support for employees who experience harassment, such as counselling services, employee assistance programs, or access to external resources?
- Does the organisation allow a support person to be present at interviews and meetings?
- Does the organisation follow up to check on health and safety and review whether the actions taken were effective?
- Does the organisation provide resources for support groups and better ombuds functions?

Questions about self-evaluation and continuous improvement, such as:

- Has the organisation established mechanisms for ongoing feedback and dialogue to address concerns and identify areas for improvement?
- Does it seek ways to improve processes and positively transform culture through education, awareness and shared responsibility and collegiality in seeking to curtail rather than conceal?

Remediation

Recognition and response go a long way toward deterring and stopping harassment. However, because organisation-level factors are the fundamental determinants of harassment, the most significant impact will be through remedial measures to improve the organisational culture that creates the conditions for harassment to thrive. Unsafe interaction among perpetrators and targets is a symptom of work environments where psychological harassment can take hold. Patriarchal, hierarchical, opaque structures; pressure to perform; and poor communication frameworks generate the atmosphere that propels the coalmine toward harmful working conditions.

The systematic failure of management to address psychological harassment is not only a matter of management avoiding accountability. It is crucial to recognise that dysfunction in the workplace often actually reinforces management power and influence. Perpetrators serve at the pleasure of management and become even more beholden to and dominated by senior management. The mindset, 'Even a bad manager is better than a whistleblower - the target is the problem,' must be replaced with a new mindset that says, 'We encourage, recognise and reward *positive* behaviours. There will be accountability for those who abuse their positions and other workers. And there will be accountability also for those who support them.'

And in cases where proper process has found that workplace psychological abuse has occurred, it is essential appropriate remedial actions are taken to address the issue to reach a place where all parties can move on. There must be appropriate processes to address wrongs, and manage and assist in implementing positive change. Experiences of harassment are variable, and every target is different. The range of outcomes that targets of abusive behaviours seek include:

- psychological safety free from humiliation, dehumanisation and future harm.

- perpetrator acceptance of responsibility, acknowledging the adverse impacts, expression of remorse, repair or reverse harm to the extent possible, and commitment to change (Leymann's work with victims revealed that chances of healing were reduced if the perpetrator went unpunished, the target was not properly supported, and the target felt that their safety was in question).

- a verbal or written warning; regular monitoring of behaviours; transfer of a worker to another work area; and/or demotion, dismissal.

- apology (if an apology can be sincerely given).

- leadership and/or communication training.

- review of workplace psychological abuse policy.

- coaching, counselling support and/or mentoring.

- information to all workers to raise the awareness of harassment.

- an opportunity to ask why this happened.

- a platform to share their stories.
- acknowledgement of their pain and suffering.
- acknowledgement that it is not their fault, that it was wrong.
- end to the shame and stigma.
- measures to regain normal patterns of interaction and sense of control.

Achieving a target's goals requires appropriate processes and skilled practitioners, and where the harassment is systemic, a culture shift. These can only be achieved with prioritisation and commitment from organisational leaders.

> *I don't want to be a victim. I want to be a healthy productive person. I don't want to have to prove that I've been damaged. I don't want to hang onto the harm. I'd like to recover, move on, resolve this reasonably, in a collaborative way, with support from my employer.*
>
> Personal diary

Perpetrators can be supported as well to relinquish aggression and abuse for more productive ways to approach relations with co-workers. Some organisations may even implement a kind of reconciliation processes where perpetrators and targets can acknowledge what has happened, and create a space to bridge differences. While far from what many workplaces currently model, such processes can create environments that enable forgiveness and engender renewed trust.

The courage to be happy at work

Bystander courage

We know that harassment largely happens because of the nature of the organisation, leadership, culture and context. We all play a part, and so the role of bystanders/co-workers is crucial to stopping harassment. We are all bystanders, and effective response to psychological harassment relies on the courage of bystanders. Targets cannot do it alone; and management often fails to respond. But a groundswell of solidarity can motivate them.

Mutually supportive practices go a long way to helping defuse uncivil behaviour. Bystanders are well-placed to call out what is happening; they can often see it better than the target, and the risk to them is lower. But still, often they do not. We know that bystander inaction (or complicity) contributes to the target's isolation, which is part of the abuse. The perpetrator counts on bystanders doing nothing to stop harassment. Bystander inaction is damaging because it signals to both the target and the perpetrator that the abusive behaviour is acceptable and that the target is somehow to blame.

As outlined in Chapter Three, bystanders may not intervene for many reasons. But as bystanders, we must trade in some of our old axioms of workplace survival and indeed set an example for management. Instead of 'It's none of our business', bystanders can participate in identifying and calling out harassing behaviours. Bystander values of collaboration and support reject the temptation to make excuses for doing nothing to help. Bystanders outnumber management and have influence, especially if they embrace that power and own it together. Not only can they support targets, but also they can build pressure to make leadership accountable. Their voices can carry weight if they use them. There is much bystanders can do to step up and embrace the power. 'Morally courageous people, as active bystanders, can make a crucial difference.'

Connection and identity with community can shift the dynamic in confronting dehumanizing behaviour. It starts with awareness, education and training. A collective understanding of what constitutes workplace psychological abuse and the organisation's policies and procedures regarding harassment will help bystanders to recognise and address emotionally abusive behaviour when they see it. Remember, 'I know it when I see it' doesn't work as a captain's call; there must be collective community standards that we all play a role in forming and acculturating. Education can also help people become aware of this responsibility and the roles they can play. Staff accidentally drawn into the psychological harassment process without understanding their role can be educated and supported in constructive responses.

Bystanders who witness harassment can calmly and assertively address the situation. If they feel safe, they might directly express concerns to the perpetrator to express how their actions affect others. Bystanders can also record instances of harassment, noting dates, times, locations, individuals involved, and descriptions of what occurs. This documentation can be invaluable if the situation needs to be escalated.

If the harassment persists, it needs to be reported. Intervening in situations of workplace psychological abuse can be challenging, and bystanders need to protect themselves. They should consider seeking guidance from HR/P&C or management and /or involving appropriate authorities but with an awareness of the underlying interests and motivations.

Compassion can mitigate the adverse effects of uncivil workplace behaviour on employee well-being. Compassion in action can improve outcomes at every stage of the process. Expressing solidarity and empathy towards the target can be a huge help, including offering a listening ear, validating their experiences, and reassuring them that they are not alone. Bystanders can also help by enlisting the support of other colleagues who may also be concerned about the harassment behaviour. There is strength in numbers, and by working together, it may be possible to form a united front and support the target.

Technology is likely to play an increasing role. Initiatives to prevent and stop harassment in other contexts can be adapted for workplaces, e.g. KiVa, a Finnish program for peer reporting that has been used successfully against harassment in schools. WorkRight23 is a New Zealand initiative for reporting about working conditions and behaviours that has recently been introduced in Australia. And there are many others.

Next time there's any opportunity to change anything, you had better know what you stand for and what you want to say.
Taylor Swift

Institutional courage

The work starts with us. A genuine, effective response is about replacing anachronistically individualistic approaches to psychological harassment and other uncivil behaviours. Moving forward positively means recognising the unhealthy dynamics and motivations and working together to replace them with better, safer practices. What is needed is shared responsibility and the sunlight to disinfect, i.e.

implementing transparent, collaborative, mutually supportive team cultures conducive to psychosocially healthy workplaces.

Because harassment is hard to fix and reinforces management power, there is a disinclination at the highest levels to undertake this transformation work. However, a groundswell of solidarity can ignite motivation for safer, more democratic workplaces where diversity is genuinely respected. Effective remediation requires this collective courage and solidarity of purpose.

Positive work environments are crucial in addressing harassment and maintaining and enhancing productivity. By promoting respect, empathy, inclusivity and effective communication, organisations can create supportive climates that encourage whole-of-workplace well-being and engagement, improving productivity and performance. Implementing robust workplace policies, raising awareness, providing support services, and promoting respect and inclusivity can mitigate the broader societal impacts of emotional abuse in the workplace. The work requires concerted efforts from various stakeholders, including organisations, policymakers, and society.

Systemic change dismantles conditions that hold problems in place. This can be done through policies, practices, and resource flows, as well as by reworking the fabric of relationships, power, dynamics, and mental models. These processes take time, commitment, thoughtful communication, education, and a gradual shift in attitudes and practices.

Like all relationships, healthy work relationships require honesty, respect and trust; 'the best people respond well to an opening bid of trust.' Courage is a cornerstone of trust. Underpinning the research on institutional courage is the understanding that the response to harassment is equally as important as the original event itself. It is not only about what happens, but also *what happens next*. Institutional betrayal is harmful, but as Jennifer Freyd explains, its antidote, institutional courage, remediates on several levels, serving as a commitment to seek truth and engage in moral action despite unpleasantness, risk, and short-term cost. Institutional courage is a pledge to protect and care for those who depend on the institution; a compass oriented to the common good of individuals, the institution, and the world; and a force that transforms workplaces into more accountable, equitable, healthy environments for everyone.

There are many ways to build healthy psychosocial work environments. Part of it is ameliorating the effects of the organisational antecedents outlined in Chapter Four, e.g. monitoring authoritarian and laissez-faire management styles, providing antidotes to unstable or high-pressure work environments, keeping a lid on organisational change, and taking steps to continuous improvement of psychosocial safety.

Organisations can move the dial toward genuine collaboration and belonging by celebrating teamwork, mutual responsibility and a more tangible, genuine commitment to shared values, demonstrating a commitment to clear moral and behavioural standards. This includes education and training for the institutional community (*especially* leadership).

Everyone in the workplace must be attentive to signs of psychological harassment, such as demeaning or belittling comments, exclusion, spreading rumours, or excessive criticism, and commit to curbing behaviour that makes others uncomfortable. This includes zero tolerance for triangulation, gossip and undermining of colleagues - at or outside of work - and training staff in appropriate, constructive ways to inform colleagues directly of issues or problems.

A culture of silence can be disrupted through processes by which skilled professionals facilitate remediation through open discussion involving multiple constituencies. Unbiased professionals from outside the system can help with remediation at the granular level, even as that system itself more broadly moves past its old habits of ignoring harassment and mobbing dynamics. Programs in the workplace to reduce retribution and recrimination and increase cooperation can also be beneficial.

Leadership courage

Management is responsible for the organisation's culture and the conditions that permit harassment to thrive. Employers who turn a blind eye are complicit in the damage created. Accountability is critical. We need our leaders to shift from seeing harassment as a problem to be denied. We need them to celebrate the achievement in overcoming psychological harassment for the dignity and well-being of all workers. Employers who recognise, respond and remediate effectively model the institutional courage to bring about the needed change.

As noted above, leaders and the entire community need to be educated about harassment and related trauma of all types. Along with employees, managers need to be trained to recognise psychologically abusive behaviours and to foster a respectful workplace culture with effective communication.

Mindful organisations regularly engage in self-study with scientifically sound anonymous surveys such as those available through platforms like WorkRight23. Institutions that regularly monitor and assess the effectiveness of anti-harassment measures can ask themselves whether they promote institutional courage, or are they still in betrayal mode? Surveys, focus groups, committees and/or anonymous feedback mechanisms can help gauge employee satisfaction, collect meaningful data, and discuss findings to identify potential issues and make necessary adjustments to policies and practices. Though it might be perceived as dangerous, this will inspire trust and repair.

There are many ways to build a healthy culture – together, we can improve things. The effort need not begin and end within the organisation. A great way to engage with the issue is to use the power of the organisation to help address the problem at a societal level. For instance, a research or educational institution can produce and disseminate knowledge about workplace emotional abuse. Or commit resources to the problem, supporting research, conferences, etc - 'Don't tell me what you value, show me your budget, and I'll tell you what you value.'

Managers in mindful, learning organisations take responsibility. Welcoming opportunities to do better, they model 'extreme ownership' and institutional courage through respectful and inclusive behaviour. They are vigilant, self-aware and courageous in helping their subordinates become better managers.

To acculturate healthy management styles and good leadership, checks and balances must be in place to moderate power structures and highly interdependent relationships. Accountability and reward for adopting supportive, authentic, transformational and fair leadership styles correlated with reduced incidence of harassment can curb the effects of authoritarian and laissez-faire management styles.

Managers in senior positions are human, too. Like everyone, they want to feel safe; they want to feel a sense of belonging. They have self-interest. But they are not selected for positions of leadership to protect their own personal positions. As leaders, it is their job to look after collective interests and put the interests of others first, including promoting safe workplaces for everyone. The distinction of good leadership is that it is the highest level of responsibility.

We repose trust in leaders to put their own interests aside. There are good leaders. But for them, perhaps even more than the rest of us, there are compelling reasons not to act. For them to expose abuse of power requires empathy, humility, selflessness, and courage. Collective courage can be inspired by leaders who are humble, honest, caring, aware, accountable, available, and supportive.

The literature on leadership is vast, with waves of new research added every year to unravel the mysteries of good leadership. Studies show that charisma, confidence, and even narcissism are often preferred in selection processes for leadership roles. It seems the discourse has created a kind of leadership idolatry that, together with an influential leadership industry, promotes the positive aspects of leadership, but not the human fallibility. Leaders themselves reinforce this with their power of messaging.

Some researchers call for more balanced perspectives and research methods about leadership to ensure credibility and legitimacy. Leadership is not a role, it is not a prize. Leadership is actually a bit like love; it not a thing, it is something people do. And because we're human and because change is constant, leadership must constantly change. And like love, when leadership goes wrong, it can be painful and costly.

Good leadership is exceptional. Freud argued that we select leaders with narcissistic tendencies as a disguised form of self-love or a substitute for our inability to love ourselves. We admire them for their strong state of mind. Perhaps, but either way, we can all cultivate strength in the entire workforce and, at the same time, expect more of our leaders. Safe workplaces may be our right, but they are also a responsibility. To make safe workplaces a reality is a responsibility we all share.

Chapter conclusion

There are many ways to build a healthy culture – together, we can improve things. Together we can support dignity at work. We can implement appropriate and effective recognition, response, and remediation of the workplace ecosystem. Together we can ensure our right to safe, healthy learning organisations that are no longer susceptible to cultures in which psychological harassment persists. If you know of an organisation like this, support it, patronise it, be a part of it. If the organisation you work for is not like this, ask why.

Selected references

Bond, S. A., Tuckey, M. R., & Dollard, M. F. (2010). Psychosocial safety climate, workplace bullying, and symptoms of posttraumatic stress. *Organization Development Journal, 28*(1), 37.

Crawshaw, L. (2013). Coaching abrasive leaders: Contradictory tales of the big bad wolf. In *Workplace Bullying* (pp. 132-148). Routledge.

Dollard, M. F., & Bakker, A. B. (2010). Psychosocial safety climate as a precursor to conducive work environments, psychological health problems, and employee engagement. *Journal of occupational and organizational psychology, 83*(3), 579-599.

Escartín, J., Ceja, L., Navarro, J., & Zapf, D. (2013). Modeling workplace bullying behaviors using catastrophe theory. *Nonlinear dynamics, psychology, and life sciences, 17*(4), 493-515.

Farr-Wharton, B., Simpson, A. V., Brunetto, Y., & Bentley, T. (2023). The role of team compassion in mitigating the impact of hierarchical bullying. *Journal of management & organization*, 1-15.

Freyd, J. J., & Smidt, A. M. (2019). So you want to address sexual harassment and assault in your organization? Training is not enough; Education is necessary. *Journal of Trauma & Dissociation, 20*(5), 489-494.

Freyd, Jennifer. (2018). Commentary: Ten steps toward institutional courage: When sexual assault victims speak out, their institutions often betray them, *The Conversation*.

Hirschman, A. O. (1972). *Exit, voice, and loyalty: Responses to decline in firms, organizations, and states*. Harvard University Press.

Karp, T. (2023). Perspective chapter: We expect effective leadership from leaders, but is this the case in reality? Reframing a much-hyped phenomenon by investigating the antithesis. In *Organisational Behavior – Negative Aspects*. Intech Open.

Leibnitz, G. M., Gillian-Daniel, D. L., Greenler, R. M. C. C., Campbell-Montalvo, R., Metcalf, H., Segarra, V. A., ... & Sims, E. L. (2022). The inclusive professional framework for societies: Changing mental models to promote diverse, equitable, and inclusive STEM systems change. *Frontiers in Sociology, 6*, 784399.

Parliament of Australia, House of Representatives Committees, House, Standing Committee on Education and Employment, Inquiry into Workplace Bullying, 2012.

Safework Australia, Dealing with Workplace Bullying – A Worker's Guide 2016.

Sloan, L. M., Matyok, T., Schmitz, C. L., & Short, G. F. L. (2010). A story to tell: Bullying and mobbing in the workplace. *International Journal of Business and Social Science, 1*(3).

Staub, Ervin. (2003). *The psychology of good and evil: Why children, adults, and groups help and harm others*. Cambridge University Press.

https://human-centered.simplecast.com/episodes/jenniferfreyd.

https://www.institutionalcourage.org/the-courage-brief-july-2022.

https://www.researchgate.net/profile/Jose_Navarro12/publication/256466911_Modeling_workplace_bullying_using_catastrophe_theory/links/547e14340cf2c1e3d2dc1920.pdf.

https://www.researchgate.net/profile/Jose_Navarro12/publication/256466911_Modeling_workplace_bullying_using_catastrophe_theory/links/547e14340cf2c1e3d2dc1920.pdf.

https://www.thevisiblevoicespodcast.com/episodes/dL8AoezxeSBUmBvTis3oVQ.

https://www.workright23.org.nz.

Epilogue

The alchemy of change

Throughout history, it has been the inaction of those who could have acted; the indifference of those who should have known better; the silence of the voice of justice, when it mattered most; that has made it possible for evil to triumph.

Haile Selassie

Psychological harassment threatens worker safety; it is too prevalent and too costly to continue to ignore. All workers have a right to a safe physical and psychosocial work environment, but there are many obstacles; effective action requires hard work and commitment.

Harassment is not conflict; it is abuse and needs to be dealt with accordingly. However, too often, targets bear the burden of stopping the perpetrator. Targets need information, education and support to respond most effectively. They need to understand that the psychological harassment they experience at the hands of the perpetrator is just the beginning. They often find management fails to support them because, perversely, psychological harassment serves management's interests in many ways. HR/P&C does not support targets and may actively or passive-aggressively work against targets because the job of HR/P&C is to protect management interests (which are not the same as the interests of the organisation).

If targets decide to stand up, speak up, and seek help, they should only do so with an awareness of the actual state of play, the realities of what they are about to face, and how the deck is stacked against them. Only then can they have a chance to take on the challenge of breaking the silence and achieving some positive change through processes of recognition, response and remediation.

Ultimately, targets cannot effect lasting change on their own. Prioritisation of the issue by management is crucial to ensuring safe work environments where harassment is not permitted to crowd out the space for healthy cultures to grow.

- The time is long overdue for organisations to retire the approach to 'Deny the problem. Speaking up threatens the status quo, incumbent power structures and reputational capital' and replace it with 'Speaking up is like having an internal consultant who helps us see what is happening. We can always change for the better. Our reputational capital and the organisation's will be stronger for it.'
- The time is long overdue for organisations to shift from 'A problem not recognised or responded to is not a problem' to 'Building a better organisation matters to us. We recognise and respond through genuine policies and procedures and build and support culture with iterative education and training processes.'
- And the time is long overdue for organisations to shift from 'Even a bad manager is better than a whistleblower; the target is the problem.' to 'This organisation models accountability for those who abuse other workers and their positions, and for those who fail to step up to their responsibilities for managing healthy teams. We recognise and reward positive behaviours.'

Workplace emotional abuse, incivility, harassment, discrimination, and coercive control are widespread, and they are emotionally, financially and socially costly. We cannot achieve healthy workplaces by paying lip service to values such as teamwork, openness, collaboration and innovation. Creating the substrate for workers to survive and thrive is essential.

Bystander support and action are also crucial to changing the patterns of abuse, but they are discouraged by tactics of denial, DARVO and outrage management. Both bystander and institutional courage are required to eradicate noxious behaviours and influences so that people can feel safe in moving away from their self-protecting survival mechanisms that block genuine respect and trust. Courage is key to supportive teamwork and collaboration to implement robust workplace policies, expand awareness and promote respect and inclusivity.

Our workplaces have great potential to be more productive, respectful, and harmonious. If being human matters, if the quality of our lives matters, there is great value in this. Could it be that the transformation we are called to now is to to give up the counter-productive struggling of 'who's on top?' and 'who's not?' and instead prioritise encouraging each other to greater collective achievement that benefits us all as individuals as well? There is so much important, urgent work to be done worldwide. How do we justify wasting our time tearing down our co-workers?

Regulators can help ensure accountability for safe workplaces, but the structural power dynamics cannot be addressed principally through legal means and government regulation. Addressing workplace psychological harassment requires concerted efforts from organisations, policymakers, and society. And it requires good leadership. There is much talk and ink spilled about the magic of leadership. It gets attention *because it is not the usual story*. Good leadership, the alchemy of a great team, is extraordinary. Maybe you have it. But it is not up to any person acting on their own to change the world. Each of us can be the change. Joining in the solidarity of courage could be a way to enjoy the fruits of success, to be happy at work.

END

Elizabeth Crawford Spencer

www.ingramcontent.com/pod-product-compliance
Lightning Source LLC
Chambersburg PA
CBHW062058290426
44110CB00022B/2641